DEVELOPING SUCCESSFUL
SPORT SPONSORSHIP PLANS
2nd Edition

Titles in the Sport Managment Library

DEVELOPING SUCCESSFUL SPORT SPONSORSHIP PLANS

2nd Edition

David K. Stotlar
University of Northern Colorado

Fitness Information Technology
•
A Division of ICPE
262 Coliseum, WVU-PE
PO Box 6116
Morgantown, WV 26506-6116

Library of Congress Card Catalog Number: 2004115255
ISBN: 1885693567

Production Editors: Geoffrey C. Fuller, Corey Madsen
Cover design: 40 West Studios
Typesetter: Jamie Pein
Printed by Sheridan Books
Printed in the United States of America

10   9   8   7   6   5   4   3   2   1

Fitness Information Technology
A Division of the International Center for Performance Excellence
262 Coliseum, WVU-PE
PO Box 6116
Morgantown, WV 26506-6116 USA
800.477.4348 (toll free)
304.293.6888 (phone)
304.293.6658 (fax)
Email: fit@fitinfotech.com
Website: www.fitinfotech.com
Cover photo © 2005, SportsChrome Inc. All rights reserved.

Dedication

I dedicate this book to my wife Sylvia. Always the one to brighten my day and lead me to appreciate life. She has been a wonderful addition to my life, adding an excitement and exuberance that keeps me on my toes. Her work in advertising and sales has also helped with my professional work, but it is her spunk that makes my day.

David Stotlar

Contents

Detailed Contents

CHAPTER 4 • *Olympic Sponsorship Opportunities*

CHAPTER 5 • *Individual Athlete Sponsorships*

CHAPTER 6 • *Financial Implications*

Preface

This workbook was developed as a companion to *Fundamentals of Sport Marketing* (Pitts & Stotlar, 2001). It evolved through several years of developing, reviewing, and critiquing sport sponsorships and draws on the author's experience in academia and the sport industry. While some discussion of sport sponsorship theory is presented in *Fundamentals of Sport Marketing*, this workbook examines the topic from the perspective of the sponsored property, rather than as a marketing tactic. It provides an overview of the theoretical underpinnings of the topic, followed by examples from actual sport sponsorships. In some cases, the name of the sport organization has been changed for reasons of confidentiality. Each section also provides worksheets for use in constructing quality sponsorship proposals.

The intent is simple: provide a workbook that assists individuals in creating a sponsorship proposal through well-defined, industry-proven protocol. A sequential process is provided to build a quality sponsorship proposal that ensures success. Enjoy the workbook and good luck in seeking sport sponsorships.

David Stotlar

Chapter One

Understanding Sport Sponsorship

Chapter Outline

Introduction

Sponsorship, in its essence, is based on a mutual exchange between a sport entity and a corporation (Copeland, Frisby, & McCarville, 1996: McCarville & Copeland, 1994). This reliance on exchange theory suggests that both entities can simultaneously provide and receive benefits. Thus, a symbiotic relationship can be attained. In the case of adidas' sponsorship of the New Zealand All Blacks rugby team, Motion, Leitch, and Brodie (2003, p. 1083) noted, "in sponsorship both the sponsor and the sponsored activity become involved in a symbiotic relationship with a transference of inherent values from the activity to the sponsor." In the United States and many other nations, sport organizations have aggressively marketed themselves to sponsors in an effort to obtain the funds necessary to operate programs. Seaver's research with 50 of the top US sponsors indicated that 10% of sponsoring companies get more than 1300 proposals per year (Seaver, 2004). U.S. 2004 sponsorship spending was projected to reach $11.4 billion, up 14% over 2003. Contributing to this total were several companies that spent over $100 million each on sponsorship programs (IEG, 2004). Among the top spending corporations:

> $250-255 million - PepsiCo
> $240-245 million - Anheuser-Busch
> $185-190 million - General Motors
> $180-185 million - Coca-Cola
> $160-165 million - Nike
> $155-160 million - Miller Brewing
> $125-130 million – Daimler-Chrysler
> $100-105 million – Ford Motor Company

The major areas of the economy where sponsorship spending was apportioned have been noted below (IEG, 2004):

> Sports - 69% ($7.69 billion)
> Entertainment - 10% ($1.06 billion)
> Festivals/Fairs - 7% ($792 million)
> Cause Marketing 9% ($ 991 million)
> Arts - 5% ($608 million)

Financial expenditures on sponsorship activities were not limited to North America. International corporate spending also escalated over 2003. European corporations contributed $7.9 billion, followed by Pacific Rim countries with $5.2 billion. Central/South America spent an additional $2.3 billion. Various other regional spending accounted for $1.5 billion, bringing the worldwide 2004 spending total to $28 billion. This figure represents an increase of 8.1% above 2003 revenues (IEG, 2004). Clearly, sponsorship represents an opportunity for the growing list of multinational companies.

There is an increasing need for sport administrators and managers to understand the methodologies of this marketing component. Sponsorship has been defined as "a cash and/or in-kind fee paid to a property (typically sports, arts, entertainment, or causes) in return for access to the exploitable commercial potential associated with that property" (Ukman, 2004a, p. 154).

Some concerns exist as to whether the sports marketing field is saturated, or if it will continue to grow in the years ahead. Many sports are heavily engaged in sponsorship (professional football, basketball, tennis and golf) while others are less involved. From high school sports to college programs to professional leagues, everyone seems to want to be involved in sport sponsorship. In 2003, the Los Angels Unified School District even conducted a workshop for potential sponsors. The potential is so great that the Carroll Independent School district in Texas hired a full-time director of sponsorships in 2003. San Antonio opted to hire an agency with the school district keeping 35% of the revenues ("A Tale of Two Districts," 2003). High schools in Texas and North Carolina went so far as to pursue naming rights for their facilities, a practice once reserved for professional teams. One high school near the Dallas-Ft. Worth airport secured $4 million from Dr. Pepper to place a logo on the school's roof that could be seen by airline passengers (Popke, 2002). At the collegiate level, about 10% of income for NCAA Division I programs come from sponsorship revenue with the average sponsorship for an NCAA Division I institution at $1.13 million (Tomasini & Stotlar, 2003).

Professional sport leagues were able to increase sponsorship revenues by 400% from 1995 - 2000. In fact, National Football League (NFL) rights fees grew 1000% between 1995 and 1998. For instance, MCI paid $1 million for its NFL sponsorship in 1997, but rival Sprint paid $24 million for similar rights during the 1998 season. Coca-Cola, on the other hand, cut its NFL sponsorship by 66%, opting instead to sign with select teams. Rival Pepsi then stepped in and signed with the league for an annual $32.5 million over 5 years through 2008. Control over the league's sponsorship is continually a topic in owners meetings. Many owners want to preserve marketing rights for the team while others, principally in small market cities, advocate league-wide sponsorships where revenues are shared equally across all teams.

In an effort to minimize the overabundance of signage inside sport stadiums some professional teams (Buffalo Bills, Portland Trail Blazers) began to segment their stadiums. This concept involved the development of sponsor zones, each dedicated to a single sponsor extending from banners on parking lot light poles to entrances, and culminating with field/court and scoreboard signage inside the facility ("Buffalo Bills look," 1996).

Park and recreation departments are also engaged in sport sponsorship activities. Beyond the longstanding traditions of sponsors for little league teams and outfield signage at the ballpark, some park and recreation mangers are exploring new ground. The City of New York signed a sponsorship agreement naming Rollerblades as their official in-line skates. Through the arrangement, Rollerblades provided free skates for security staff and offered free skating and roller hockey clinics in various NYC parks. Rollerblades also received special signage on the sides of security vehicles in Central Park (A.R.C., 1998).

What initially attracted sponsors to sport is the ability to reach consumers in a less cluttered environment than traditional advertising (Cordiner, 2002a). The clutter in advertising is such that the average consumer is exposed to over 5,000 messages every day. Sponsorship had the potential to deliver advertising messages more effectively than established advertising channels. However, sport may now have become over-saturated. According to Amshay and Brian (1998) many sport events have become "cluttered with title sponsors, presenting sponsors, supporting sponsors, cam-sponsors, official product sponsors, pouring rights, licensing rights, ad nauseam. . . .Clutter and dilution are in direct opposition to what sponsors want" (p. 23). In a cluttered market, many sponsors are seeking alternatives to mainstream sport, moving instead to action or extreme sports. Not only have they found these markets less cluttered, but the events have a strong psychographic pull with 18-24 year-old consumers (Cordiner, 2002b).

Several authorities note sponsors are changing their strategy for sponsorship. The emerging theme is "Fewer, bigger, better." Poole (2003, p. 14) said that sponsors "would rather spend more money on bigger properties than spread their sponsorships around to more numerous, smaller properties." In 2004, the Tampa Bay Buccaneers moved to a "less is more" stance for their sponsorship. Their goal was to reduce clutter and provide better service to their marketing partners by limiting the total number of sponsors. A similar trend was seen at the 2002 World Cup in soccer where the number of sponsors was reduced from 43 in France '98 to 28, 15 partners plus official suppliers and licensees. Seaver's 2004 corporate survey revealed the same direction. One executive commented, "We are doing fewer programs in the coming year; however, the programs that we're staying with will be bigger and better." Another said, "what we'll be doing we'll be doing at a higher level. Big impact is better for us, we feel, than a lot of small sponsorships. This will affect the second-tier sports and the number of people we will be talking to" (Seaver, 2004, p. 20).

The issue of clutter also affects the methods that sponsors choose to communicate with consumers. Researchers at an event in Holland found that some sponsors were labeled "un-cool" because their presence was too obvious, while sponsors that had relevant activation were perceived more favorably. According to Ukman (2003, p. 2) "there is a huge gap between how marketers want to reach people and how people want to be reached." Sponsorship can bridge that gap.

Sponsorship Background

In the early history of sport marketing, sponsorship activities often served the interests of corporate CEO's ("Let's sponsor golf, because I like golf."). This allowed company executives to mix socially with elite athletes and also provide client entertainment activities. However, these rationales have almost disappeared in the modern era of sport sponsorship. Nevertheless, most major sporting events continue to provide hospitality areas as part of sponsorship packages where executives can meet with celebrity-athletes before and after the competition. Notwithstanding these possibilities, greater sophistication evolved after the 1980s and 1990s.

There has been a considerable amount of debate about whether companies engage in sponsorship activities for philanthropic reasons or for financial benefits. Moreover, an interesting new term was recently introduced into the realm of business management. *strategic philanthropy* has been defined as "a company's long-term investment in an appropriate cause that does measurable good in society while enhancing the company's reputation with key audiences" (Jones, 1997, p. 33). In 2004, IEG began conducting seminars called Strategic Philanthropy for its corporate clients. The seminars focused on "Leveraging Philanthropy with Marketing" and "Putting Hope and Heart into Sales" (Strategic Philanthropy, 2004). Social responsibility has been an aspect of corporate philosophy for many years and numerous sport causes have benefited. Many art, cultural, sport, medical, and social programs have been assisted by corporate giving. However, corporate motives must be examined. Have companies engaged in philanthropy for altruistic reasons, or self-interest?

Research has shown that consumers are influenced by a company's charitable activities. It has been found that 14% of consumers sought out companies with viable corporate philanthropy programs and 40% saw a company's corporate citizenship as a tie-breaker when deciding which company to patronize (Jones, 1997). Research also shows that the overlay of a cause can lead to increased purchase intent if there is little difference between brands on quality and price. However, the positive effects of cause-related marketing appear to diminish as the difference in competing brands increases (Roy & Graeff, 2003). There are many corporations that tie sport and cause-related marketing together. Verizon Wireless sponsors a team of professional women cyclists who volunteer to give any winnings to HopeLine (Verizon's initiative to help victims of domestic violence). They also created a program through HopeLine and the Chicago Cubs called "Safe at Home." Verizon and the Cubs collected used wireless phones at the Verizon Wireless kiosk/booth inside Wrigley Field and the used wireless handsets, batteries and accessories (from any carrier) were refurbished, recycled, and provided for victims of domestic violence. In addition, Verizon donated $25 for every double a Cubs player hit during the season to Cubs Care, to support domestic violence shelters in Chicago. Verizon also served as the title sponsor of the Cubs wives "Cubs Care" event that raised $100,000 for area shelters through an auction and photo opportunities with Cubs players. The Cubs community relations department also provided home-games tickets to the clients and staff of 15 domestic violence shelters in Chicago.

While it seems (in the opinion of the author) ludicrous, some corporate officers talk about "owning a cause" (Jones, 1997, p. 36). This does not sound like true philanthropy, but perhaps more like marketing strategy. According to Jones (1997, p. 34), "it [doesn't] take long for consumers to see these tactics as sales pitches thinly veiled in the guise of social activism."

Granted, there may be corporations that engage in sport sponsorship for truly philanthropic reasons. However, the record shows that charitable approaches have limited success in securing corporate sponsorships. Corporate self-interest has been considerably more viable as a motivation for involvement with sport sponsorship.

A closer look at the reasons why businesses would be attracted to sport is detailed in Chapter 3. Some of the more prominent justifications reveal that sport is attractive to sponsors because it can provide a cross-sectional demographic exposure when compared to other marketing avenues. The diverse demographics represented by many sport activities and events is crucial to corporations and thus, to the creation of potential sponsorship affiliations.

Sponsoring sport often adds a double exposure for sponsors with on-site promotional activities and media coverage. For example, Tiger Woods appeared on the cover of *Sports Illustrated* four times within 1 1/2 years after winning his first Masters. He also adorned the covers of *Fortune* and *Business Week* (Lombardo, 1998). One sport marketer commented that you could buy the back page of *Sports Illustrated*, but you couldn't buy the front.

In yachting, an interesting incident occurred when a Finnish boat, which had secured a sponsorship agreement just one day before a major international race, obtained significant exposure for its sponsor even though it capsized during the race. The overturned boat was in range of television and news cameras and appeared on networks and newspaper front pages worldwide displaying the sponsor's name. Although it was not the type of publicity that the sponsor had in mind, people around the globe turned their newspapers up side down to read the sponsor's name on the side of the boat.

Dependence on Sponsorship

There are some authorities that believe that sport has become overly dependent on corporate sponsors to meet expenses. Three examples show that too much dependence on sponsors could have disastrous effects. In China, an international badminton tournament was canceled when sponsors pulled out during Asia's economic downturn. The Chicago stop on the Women's Tennis Association (WTA) tour was also canceled when IMG (International Management Group) could not secure a title sponsor. Further evidence was seen when a planned Women's World Doubles Championship in Fort Lauderdale was called off because the potential sponsors withdrew at the last minute.

Dependence on sponsorship monies is also evident with colleges and universities reliant on corporations and sponsorship revenues for additional income. Nike has an all-sport agreement with 20 programs while adidas has deals with six. One of the top programs in collegiate sport, the University of Michigan, receives $35 million (over 7 years) from Nike (Lee, 2003). The types of benefits currently realized by many educational institutions:
    1. Free equipment
    2. Stadium advertising
    3. Supplements to coaches' salaries
    4. Television revenues for regular and post-season games

Colleges and universities in the U.S. have realized profits in the millions of dollars from corporate sponsored football bowl games. The Bowl Championship Series games payout figures have been staggering. For 2004, the per-team BCS bowl game (Tostitos Fiesta Bowl, FedEx Orange Bowl, Nokia Sugar Bowl, and the Rose Bowl) payouts were between $14 –17 million Pedersen (2004).

In an attempt to gain greater control over sponsorship, the NCAA (as have the NFL, MLB, NHL, and NBA) has imposed rules regarding the size of corporate logos that can be displayed on team uniforms and equipment because of overt commercialization. However, in a recent lawsuit against the NCAA, apparel companies questioned the NCAA's motives when the bowl game corporate sponsors were allowed to place logos that exceeded the legal size limits on uniforms during the post-season games.

Major League Baseball also implemented rules about the size of logos on bats after the 1990 All Star Game when a player held his bat up to the camera to display its over-sized logo (ski racers have been known to do the same thing at the end of a race). The National Football League (NFL) and the National Hockey League (NHL) created significant controversy by controlling the display of logos on player apparel. Their regulations state that manufacturers must pay the league a fee for the right to display their marks during a game. Thus, an NFL player who has an endorsement deal (more on that in Chapter 5) cannot display a corporate logo on his shoes, if the shoe company has not paid the league a rights fee. To illustrate the height to which this controversy has risen, the NFL threatened in 1998 to fine Bronco players Shannon Sharpe and Bill Romanowski because they were wearing logos of EAS (Experimental and Applied Sciences, a nutritional supplement company) in the locker room. The players contended that they had the right to wear items of their choice once they left the field (Gotthelf, 1998).

Major League Baseball has not operated without controversy in this area. In 1998, MLB owners relinquished their rights to sign exclusive team agreements with uniform shoe manufacturers. Previously, each individual team could sign with a single company (e.g., adidas with the New York Yankees). However, in an out-of-court legal settlement, the uniform rights for all teams now reside with Major League Baseball Properties. In another control-oriented issue, the Baltimore Orioles attempted to stop three players from promoting Pepsi products because the team had an agreement with Coca-Cola (King & Bernstein, 1998).

The question at hand appears to be, who has the right to control—the player or the league? Similarly, the NFL has for many years packaged league-wide sponsorships. In 1998, the league was unable to negotiate a league-wide agreement with Coca-Cola and relinquished the soft drink category to the individual teams. As a result, Coke signed 16 individual teams compared to Pepsi's three (other teams remained without a soft drink sponsor). Thus, Coke was able to reduce its NFL sponsorship costs to $4 million, as opposed to the league-wide costs of $15 million from the previous year. In addition, Coke was able to strategically select markets where the sponsorships would be most effective. Unfortunately for many teams, their income was less than it had been in the preceding year. The league did, however, create two new categories of "Quick Serve Restaurant" and "Pizza," which teams could also sell (Bernstein, 1998a).

Creating Win-Win Strategies

Sports activities and corporations can create symbiotic relationships that are greater than the sum of the separate entities. Ukman (2004b, p. 2) reported, "combining the assets of allied organizations creates sponsorship platforms in which the whole is worth more than the sum of the individual parts." Sport managers want to increase their revenues and the exposure of their programs. Coincidentally, sport sponsors want to increase their revenues and the exposure of their products. A sport sponsorship arrangement can fulfill these needs for each organization. The special events manager at NutraSweet claimed that sports marketing becomes marketing at its best when event organizers and sponsors meet each other's needs ("A Sense," 1990). In general, corporations are interested in marketing their products and services to potential customers. If sport can provide a vehicle for this endeavor, then a successful relationship can be established. The task for the sport marketing professional is to make it clear to the sponsor just how this can be accomplished through his or her organization or event.

Controversies

Not everyone agrees that involvement with corporate sponsorships is good for sport. Sport marketers should, therefore, be aware that not all members of the community embrace their involvement with certain corporate sponsors. Many feel that blending alcohol and tobacco with the healthful benefits of sports is hypocritical and there have been several moves on the part of government entities and regulating bodies to restrict alcohol and tobacco advertising in sport settings.

Tobacco and Alcohol Sponsorship

Considerable debate surrounded a European Union ban on tobacco advertising in sport. The French government has had a ban in place for many years and has been pushing the application of legislation throughout Europe. The restrictions on tobacco sponsorship in sport vary across Europe. In the United Kingdom, the ban will go into effect in 2006. The German government contended that smoking was a health issue and therefore should be within the control of individual nations ("Germany to tangle," 1998). Most of the alcohol and tobacco sponsorships have eroded in Europe although the heavy dependence of Formula One racing on tobacco sponsorship is the exception. This has led some organization executives to plan for races at venues in countries more sympathetic to tobacco advertising (Currie, 2004). Formula One was at the center of the controversy following the French government's ban on tobacco advertising in sport events. In retaliation to the ban, FISA officials dropped the French Grand Prix from its schedule of events because the French Auto Sports Federation could not guarantee that police would not impound cars and equipment displaying tobacco advertising.

The Australian government adopted legislation to restrict tobacco advertising, but the regulations allow events of "international significance" to apply for an exemption. The Canadian government also enacted legislation (Bill, C71) that restricted the display of tobacco advertising in sport. "As of June 1998, sport and cultural groups got a five-year reprieve from the government's tough tobacco advertising restrictions (Danylchuk, 1998, p. 6). Existing signage would be allowed to remain through 2000 and from 2000-2003 advertising by tobacco companies was limited to on-site displays and relegated to the bottom 10% of the sign (Danylchuk, 1998)

The French, Canadian, and Australian governments are but a few of those taking action on the issue. There may be many more in waiting, including measures in the United States resulting from the negotiated settlement between various States and the tobacco industry addressing payments for medical coverage for smokers.

In 1991, the Federal Trade Commission (FTC) entered the debate surrounding tobacco and sport sponsorship. The case, *Federal Trade Commission (FTC) v. Pinkerton Tobacco Company* (1991) may have substantially changed the rules of the sport sponsorship game for tobacco companies. In this case, the Federal Trade Commission joined the battle to enforce a Federal Communication Commission (FCC) ban on television advertising of tobacco products. The case involved Pinkerton Tobacco Company's use of sporting events to advertise their Red Man brand smokeless tobacco. The results of the case yielded "cease and desist" orders outlining the methods used by Pinkerton which were in violation of FTC and FCC regulations. Furthermore, it forbade them from producing "program identifiers which appeared at the beginning or the end or before or after commercial breaks [that] include the Red Man Indian head logo." The ruling also prohibited the use of a brand name of a smokeless tobacco product as the name of a sponsored event if "the logo, selling message color, or design feature of the product or its packaging" was used. Other restrictions included a ban on the use of the above-mentioned advertising on signage in the area on which cameras routinely focus: on arena/stadium signage, on competing vehicles or other equipment or on clothing of event officials, commentators, competitors, or participants. Furthermore, Pinkerton would "be liable for civil penalties in the amount provided by law for each violation of the order (FTC v. Pinkerton Tobacco Company, 1991, p. 3)

Marlboro brand cigarettes and other tobacco companies successfully avoided television bans on tobacco advertising by purchasing advertising location in numerous stadiums and racetrack locations that appeared as background when an event was televised. Cigarette companies have had ads in numerous major league stadiums in the United States. At Fenway Park in Boston, the Marlboro sign hung in right field along with a sign for the Jimmy Fund cancer research charity. According to DeParle (1989, p. 38), "the networks have been perfectly happy to show an infield decked with Marlboro banners and race cars painted with Marlboro logos—while pretending that cigarette ads are still banned from the air." However, the Federal Trade Commission recently joined the assault to enforce FCC ban on television advertising of tobacco products. The FCC, through the US Justice Department, issued a restraining order in 1998 prior to the NFL Super Bowl to restrict TV coverage of cigarette advertising locations in the stadium that would have appeared as background for TV cameras.

In 1998, several States worked toward settlement with major tobacco companies related to health costs resulting from smoking tobacco. Part of the proposed agreement restricted all tobacco sponsorship of sporting events by the end of 2001. Any sponsorship agreement in place prior to August 2, 1998, could be retained, but not renewed. Preliminary interpretation of the settlement "allows tobacco companies to tie into one series, event, or team sanctioned by a single organization (Landmark settlement, 1998, 1). Although not precluded by the agreement, R. J. Reynolds' dropped their sponsorship of NASCAR's Winston Cup series in 2004. Substantially more inspection of the settlement will be made. Definitions and restrictions are rather vaguely worded and few details were specified regarding what a "brand" entails. In many foreign countries (although prohibited in the US agreement), tobacco manufacturers have diversified their product lines to include logos non-tobacco consumer products. This begs the question: How could you restrict Marlboro from adverting "Adventure Gear" in print and electronic outlets? The current US agreement applies the same restrictions to consumer products if a tobacco "brand name" (e.g., Winston) is used, but does not disallow use of the parent corporation (i.e., R. J. Reynolds) identity. The settlement also eliminates "brand" sponsorship of stadiums and arenas in the States covered by the agreement ("Landmark settlement," 1998).

The controversy of beer advertising has not been as well publicized as that concerning tobacco. In 1998, Carlsberg Beer negotiated and signed a contract to become a sponsor of the XVI Commonwealth Games in Malaysia. However, public pressures from the predominately Muslim society led the government to intervene.

As a result, government officials forbade the games organizers from displaying any of Carlsberg's logos on event materials or exhibiting event signage during the competition. Carlsberg was compelled to file litigation to recover its expenditures.

Virtual Signage

Virtual signage has been one of the recent developments that challenge both sport marketers and event owners. The technology behind virtual signage "allows a broadcaster to electronically insert an image—generally an advertisement—onto any one-color surface, including a playing field or boundary" (Bernstein, 1998b, p. 24). A variety of sport organizations allow for use of this technology while others restrict or prohibit its use. The National Basketball Association (NBA) has not allowed virtual signage yet it is used extensively in Major League Baseball (MLB) and the National Hockey League (NHL). The NFL is still developing a policy on the issue. Other sports have also explored the use of this new technology. The World Wrestling Federation, the X-Games, and various professional tennis tournaments have experimented with virtual signage. The controversy centers around control of the images that are presented on the field. Many facility owners convinced sponsors to purchase stadium advertising with the idea that these signs would be seen on television. However, with this technology, not only could existing stadium advertising be blocked out, but a competitor's advertising could be inserted via this computer technology. One Major League Soccer executive commented, "the stadium takes a position that they have some proprietary interest in [virtual signage], our position is that they don't" (Bernstein, 1998b, p. 24). The San Diego Padres also ran into a disagreement when the broadcaster of its games began selling virtual signage during telecasts of home contests. The following year, the Padres specified in their broadcast contract that the team, not the broadcaster, would have the rights to any virtual signage inserted into Padres games (Bernstein, 1998b).

Another point of contention has been the inclusion of sponsor signage in video games. Electronic Arts, one of the leading producers of video games, has used the marketing theme "if it's in the game, it's in the game." To this point they have included outfield signage in their MLB games, but have taken the concept to a higher level in their X-Games Pro Boarder game. This interactive game for the Sony Play Station includes prominent on-screen graphics featuring event sponsor Mountain Dew. Similarly, Gillette, sponsor of soccer's World Cup '98, was conspicuous in Electronic Arts' World Cup video game. Another video game producer, Sierra On-line, made sure to get permission to recreate corporate logos for its NASCAR video game (Rovell, 1998). Many sport marketers feel that these actions present an excellent opportunity to market to children in an authentic environment. EA Sports Director of Sports Marketing commented that "video games are a perfect vehicle for companies to target an attentive teenage audience" (EA Sports, 1998). There are, however, others who believe that this step represents another intrusion into the society that is unconscionable.

In summary, the relationship between sport organizations and sponsors must include advantages to both parties. This win-win situation can provide market value and increased profits for corporations and increased operating revenues for sport organizations and events. An overall view of the sponsorship process is provided in the Best Practice section that follows. The task for a sport marketing professional, is to make it clear to the sponsor just how this can be accomplished through your a particular sport organization or event.

Best Practice

Sponsorship Evaluation Model

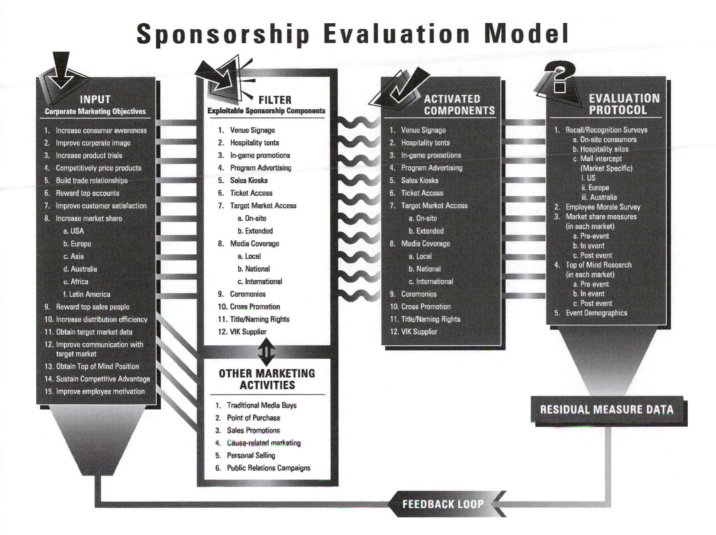

References

A sense of where you are. (1990, March). *Athletic Business*, 18.

A Tale of two districts: Texas schools take a different approach to sponsorship (2003). Retrieved November 17 from http://www.sponsorship.com/iegsr/2003/11/17/2003/4704.asp?

Amshay, T., and Brian, V. (1998, July 20-26). Sport sponsorship sword cuts both ways. *Sports Business Journal*, 23.

A.R.C. (1998, May). Sponsorship park & roll. *Athletic Business*, 18.

Bernstein, A. (1998a, September 14-20). Teams scramble for sponsorship. *Sport Business Journal*, 1,5.

Bernstein, A. (1998b, June 22-28). High tech a [virtual] sign of the times. *Sport Business Journal*, 24,36.

Buffalo Bills look to increase signage revenue by creating quadrant sponsorships in Rich Stadium. (1996, June). *Team Marketing Report*, 1, 7.

Copeland, R., Frisby, W., and McCarville, R. (1996). Understanding the sport sponsorship from a corporate perspective. *Journal of Sport Management*, 10, 1, 32-48.

Cordiner, R. (2002a, June-July). Boxing and sponsorship: A mismatch of a knockout combination. *International Journal of Sports Marketing and Sponsorship*, 175-181.

Cordiner, R. (2002b, January). Sponsors of the wide world of sport—what's in it for them? *Sports Marketing*, p.14-16.

Currie, N. (2004, March). Interview with Nigel Currie, joint chairman European Sponsorship Association. *International Journal of Sports Marketing and Sponsorship*, 246-251.

Danylchuk, K. (1998). *Sponsorship of the LPGA du Maurier Classic: Will it go up in smoke?* Gold Coast, Australia: Conference of the Sport Management Association of Australia and New Zealand.

DeParle, J. (1989, September). Warning: Sports stars may be hazardous to your health. *Washington Monthly*, pp. 34-48.

EA Sports gives teams and sponsors numerous options for video games. (1998, March). *Team Marketing Report*, 6, 1998

Germany ready to tangle over tobacco ban, (1998, July 20-26). *Sports Business Journal*, 21.

Gotthelf. (1998, September 21-27). EAS supplements its list of endorsers with signing of Buc's Alstott. *Sports Business Journal*, 15.

IEG (2004). Sponsorship spending to increase 8.7% in 2004. *IEG Sponsorship Report 22*, (24), 1, 4-5.

Jones, P. D. (1997, January). Better to give and to receive. *Hemispheres*, 33-38.

King, B., and Bernstein, A. (1998, April 27 - May 3). Teams lose logo rights in shoe deals. *Sports Business Journal*, 1, 53.

Landmark settlement restricts tobacco marketers to one brand deal per year. (1998, November 23). *IEG Sponsorship Report*, 1-2.

Lee, J. (2003, September 22-28). College deals build brand and relationships. *Sports Business Journal*, 25.

Lombardo, J. (1998a, May 4-10). 'Team Tiger' takes Woods to the top. *Sports Business Journal*, 22-23.

McCarville, R., and Copeland, B. (1994). Understanding sport sponsorship through exchange theory. *Journal of Sport Management*, 8, 2, 102-114.

Motion, J., and Leitch, S., and Brodie, R. (2003). Equity in corporate co-branding. *European Journal of Marketing*, 37, (7/8), 1080-1094.

Pedersen, P. (2004, February 1). Bowl games a big economic score for local communities. *Treasure Coast Business Journal*, 14.

Poole, M. (2003, October 27 – November 2). It's a new sponsorship world and agencies can thrive if they adapt. *Sports Business Journal*, 14.

Popke, M. (2002, October). Your name here. *Athletic Business*, 42-44.

Roy, D., and Graeff, T. (2003). Consumer attitudes toward cause-related marketing activities in professional sport. *Sport Marketing Quarterly*, 12, (3) 163-172.

Rovell. (1998, September 14-20). Sports video games an untapped market. *Sports Business Journal*, 37.

Seaver, R. (2004). *2004 Corporate Sponsorship Survey Report*. San Diego: Seaver Marketing Group.

Strategic philanthropy: building social capital and financial returns (2004). Retrieved June 28, 2004 from http://www.sponsorship.com/sproducts/109_product_agenda.asp.

Tomasini, N., and Stotlar, D. (2003). *Corporate Sponsorship Differences between Division I-A, I-AA, and I-AAA institutions*. Sport Marketing Association Annual Conference, Gainesville, FL.

Ukman (2003, December 22). Assertions. *IEG Sponsorship Report*, 22, (24), 2.

Ukman, L. (2004b, May 3). Assertions. *IEG Sponsorship Report*, 23, (8), 1-3.

Ukman, L. (2004a). *Return on Sponsorship*. Chicago: International Events Group.

Sponsorship Worksheets

The worksheets provide a guide developing various sections of a sponsorship plan. The following sheets cover possible corporate rationale for sponsorship, legal restrictions and possible controversies. Complete these worksheets as a preparatory step in the creation of a sponsorship plan.

Ascertain possible rationale that corporations may possess for sponsorship of your team, organization, or event.

_____

_____

_____

_____

_____

_____

_____

_____

Discuss any legal restrictions (i.e. tobacco/alcohol) that would affect the sponsorship of your team, organization, or event.

_____

_____

_____

_____

_____

_____

_____

_____

_____

Consider any possible controversies that may influence sponsorship of your team, organization, or event.

_____

_____

_____

_____

_____

_____

_____

_____

_____

Chapter Two

Prospecting for Sponsors

Chapter Outline

Identifying Sponsors

Involvement with sporting events and sports organizations is not the right partnership for everyone. In an off-handed comment at a national forum on sport sponsorships, one presenter joked in light of legal troubles incurred at the 2002 Winter Olympic Games that some law firm should become the official legal counsel for the International Figure Skating federation. Some things don't always fit. On the other hand, 2004 marked the first year that the Super Bowl named an official law firm. Winstead, Sechrest and Minick worked with the Houston organizing committee from the bid process through the entire contract negotiations with the league and vendors.

Not all businesses in a community have the ability or the interest to buy into sport sponsorships. However, some companies have been identified with a very natural fit to sport sponsorship. A more natural fit can be seen in San Francisco-based Gap apparel maker's sponsoring outfield signage to the left and right of center field (in baseball terms, the *gaps*). Another natural match evidenced some creativity by sport marketers. Colorado State University's mascot is a Ram, so coming off a successful year in football, they acquired Dodge trucks as a sponsor of their coach's show to promote its popular Ram trucks. Gatorade, developed in 1965 by University of Florida doctors to help re-hydrate their football players has been a staple on NFL and college sidelines for 35 years. When the TV audience sees a Gatorade cooler on the field, they know that the product works. Pepsi (owner of the Gatorade brand) extended its sponsorship with the NFL through 2011.

Sport marketer, finds those businesses that have both an interest and the ability to participate. Sponsorship pioneer David Wilkinson said, "Make no mistake. The process of finding sponsors and then showing them how you can help them requires imagination and marketing effort" (Wilkinson, 1986, p. 40). As a starting place, sport marketers research the current trends within individual business sectors. Articles and trade publications are often great sources for information on corporate activity. Simply reading the business section of a local paper is a convenient place to begin. If dealing with the prospect of national sponsorships, the nation's leading business sources like the *Wall Street Journal* are a useful resource. Looking for information on corporate mergers, business expansion, and product launches can be profitable. When financial services giant Wachovia merged with First Union in 2001 they embarked on a massive sponsorship campaign across the northeast securing a variety sponsorship rights and teams deals. Through the merger, the First Union Center in Philadelphia became the Wachovia Center. In 2004, package and express delivery firm DHL was expanding its network across the US. Long known for its international services, DHL aimed at stealing market share from FedEx and UPS. They struck a deal with the USOC just prior to the 2004 Athens Olympic Games and through that association bought exclusive advertising packages on NBC during the Games.

In another example, the Boston Marathon brought in the Mercedes car group (a unit of Daimler Chrysler) for the 2004 race and its launch of the "smart" brand. The race offered substantial media exposure and 500,000 on-course spectators. Smart brand executives noted, "Smart drivers have a lot in common with marathon runners. They are more active than average and have a variety of interests. They have a zest for life, a great deal of enthusiasm and do not define themselves by age and social background, but by intellectual and creative potential. The smart brand will offer products that appeal to this audience in the United States" (Smart brand vehicles, 2004). Noting business activity like this certainly adds to the possibilities of finding sponsors who could benefit from a sport marketing platform. Other examples were evident in 2004 when Atlantic Coast Airlines re-branded itself as Independence Air. The Washington Redskins (NFL) secured them as a sponsor to help them communicate their new name and to promote their east coast routes (Ukman, 2004).

Access to this type of information also comes through sport sponsorship trade publications. Trade publications in the sport business field such as IEG Sponsorship Report and Sports Business Journal are valuable sources of information. IEG Sponsorship Report regularly publicizes the most active categories involved in sponsorship. For the year ending in 2003, the most active companies were nonalcoholic beverages (where 44% of properties had one as a sponsor), automotive (with 35%), banks (30%), beer (29%), telecommunications (26%), specialty retail (19%), food (18%), and financial services (14%) (IEG, 2003). Therefore, companies in these economic sectors may be likely candidates to approach for sponsorship.

Castiglione (1989) indicated that the local Chamber of Commerce is also a good source of information for analysis. The local Chamber of Commerce records typically include business profiles covering personnel, financial base, and company products. Other sources suggested by Wilkinson (1986) include looking through the Yellow Pages of the telephone book, examining ads in the newspaper, and simply taking a drive through the business district to stimulate the imagination in creating a potential match. Another technique that has proven successful is to examine specific business relations of a sport organization or institution. There may be some natural relationships that would be strengthened through a sponsorship agreement. Many times businesses that do business with have a vested interest in a marketer's success.

Perhaps the best example of this concept is the enormously successful sponsorship of Hendrick Racing by DuPont. Understanding the circumstances shows that Hendrick owns more than 90 automotive dealerships with over $2.5 billion in annual revenues. Each of these dealerships maintains a collision repair facility, which purchases a massive amount of automotive paint. DuPont Automotive Finishes happens to be one of the leading retailers of automotive paint. Thus, Hendrick gained sponsorship of its racecar, driven by Jeff Gordon, and DuPont gained product sales and significant other benefits through the relationship (Hagstrom, 1998). In a similar move, Sherwin-Williams entered into a partnership with the Big South Conference as the official paint supplier for 2004. "The partnership will allow Sherwin-Williams the opportunity to claim a strong foothold in a League that spends a large sum on paint and supplies each year" ("Sherwin-Williams," 2004). Although not specifically mentioned, the relationship will allow Sherwin-Williams access to the entire University system that buys more paint than just the athletic program.

As a follow-up step, the reader should generate a list of businesses and corporations assessing the criteria delineated in Chapter 3. Thereafter, rank the potential for each business listed as a starting place for sponsor prospecting.

Finding the correct point of access is often difficult. Some retail outlets arrange their own sponsorship agreements, while in other situations; sponsorships are administered from corporate headquarters. Many local businesses are affiliated with franchises and chains of similar stores (such as Pizza Hut, McDonalds, True Value Hardware Stores, etc.). If some cases, the marekerter may need to go through the corporate headquarters for approval. This is not always a disadvantage, as the main corporation may have more money to commit than does a local retailer, and corporate executives may be willing to utilize ideas to promote the entire company. Regardless of where the final decision is made, a sport marketer should always visit with the local franchise owner/distributor first. If a sport marketer attempts to find a sponsor without at least tacit support from a local retailer, chances of success will be diminished. The Coors Beer example (in the Best Practice section at the end of this chapter) shows how the costs for sponsorship on some ventures were set up on a cooperative, shared-cost basis (more detail on corporate access will be provided in Chapter 8).

Before asking a corporate sponsor what their business objectives are, research the following questions:

1. What type of product or service does the corporation produce?
2. What is their marketing structure?
3. What are their general marketing approaches?
4. What types of programs are successful?
5. Where does the corporation stand versus their competition?
6. Have they used sports/events previously and, if so, was their experience positive or negative?
7. Who makes their marketing decisions?

(List adapted from Wilkinson, 1986)

Investigating Potential Sponsors

One of the keys to success is the ability to investigate the sponsoring company. Do the homework! The first step in investigating a corporation is gaining access to their corporate literature, such as their annual report. Begin by requesting the annual report directly from the corporate office; though many companies also post their annual report on their web site. The SEC (Securities & Exchange Commission) requires all publicly held companies in the US with over 500 shareholders and $10 million in assets to file annual reports. Information in these reports can be accessed through the SEC's web site (www.sec.gov) and through Public Register's Annual Report Service (www.prars.com). These documents will tell a lot about the inner workings of the target companies. There are, however, many things that a company doesn't want the public and their shareholders to know that the sport marketer needs to know. For this perspective, read clippings from area newspapers, or talk to people who do business with the company. Just knowing who holds what office is not enough, to the sport marketer must know who the power brokers are in the corporation.

The process also involves a thorough investigation of the sponsor's business structure. A sport marketer cannot possibly convince a sponsor that they are working in a sponsor's best interests without fully comprehending that sponsor's business. The senior marketing manager for Gulf States Toyota said, "The most critical tactic for a property that wants to work with us is to show us that they understand our business." "It would go a long way in my eyes to know that a property had talked to dealers and sales people before even talking to me" (Williamson, 2004).

A sport marketer's research should also investigate corporate ownership. In today's business world, the complexity of ownership means that companies you may be approaching have strong national and international ties. Pizza Hut, Kentucky Fried Chicken and Taco Bell were, for many years, owned by PepsiCo (now affiliated operations). Would McDonald's become involved in a sponsorship that also included Pepsi? This would most likely never happen, because of the strong ties between Coke and McDonald's through their restaurant association and their Olympic sponsorship alliance.

In many instances, a sport organization's financial partners may also serve as potential sponsors. First USA Bank is the third largest issuer of credit cards in US (currently over $1 trillion business). Some organizations such as the National Football League and Major League Baseball have successfully associated themselves with national banking conglomerates to issue Affinity Cards. These credit cards feature NFL or MLB team logos, providing increased incentive for their customers to choose a bank's card, while benefiting the sport organization or league. Through these partnerships, the sport organization receives a set payment per subscriber and a percentage of sales generated from card use.

As noted earlier, the search for sponsors can be demanding and involve significant hours of research and investigation. However, it can also be a lot of fun and present a challenge that could motivate the best and the brightest sport marketers.

Best Practice

Adolph Coors Company
Sports Sponsorship Criteria

Here are Coors criteria and rules for the Sports, CO-OP Events, Regional Events, and Special Marketing areas within the Field Marketing Department.

SPORTS
To qualify for sponsorship with Sports, subject sponsorship must meet the majority of the following guidelines:

1. Must rank high on the beer drinker index survey—participant, spectator, and viewer.
2. Must score high on the sports calculus—a calculation encompassing everything from size of audience to amount of product sold to retailer involvement opportunities.
3. Must affect the bulk of the Coors marketing territory—via on-site appearances.
4. Must fulfill the expectations or guarantee of national media coverage.
5. Individuals sponsored must be known and respected throughout Coors market area by media and spectators as a "leader" in their sport.
6. Event sponsored must be unique, contain the possibility of Coors "ownership," be directed toward our target market, be on the upswing in pop-

ularity, and provide the Coors distributors with opportunity for tie-ins.

7. Sport must also lend itself to solid consumer promotion possibilities—outreach.

8. Sport must lend itself to the process of continuity—meaningful reach as well as optimal frequency.

9. Must be controlled by a viable sanctioning body (e.g., NASCAR) that establishes or designates all events.

10. Events of sponsored party (venue) must be competitive in nature.

CO-OP EVENTS (between Distributor and Brewery)

The following rules have been established by the CO-OP Administration to ensure uniform guidelines for all Coors distributors. These rules provide distributors and departments within the company a summary of the CO-OP Administration operating latitude. Any questions not covered by these guidelines should be discussed with CO-OP Administration management.

1. Funding for programs will be shared on a 50 percent distributor/50 percent brewery basis.

2. Programs must have a minimum total cost of $1,000 to be considered for funding.

3. Program must be in compliance with applicable laws and regulations.

4. Programs must be in conformance with the company marketing plan, marketing strategy, and corporate image.

5. Programs must be submitted on the authorized CO-OP Event proposal form with sufficient information to allow thorough analysis and evaluation.

6. Program proposals should be received by the area sales manager at least 30 days prior to the program start date, 60 days if special graphics will be required.

7. Proposals submitted after program completion may be declined.

8. Co-sponsorships with other beer companies are not allowed.

9. Use of Coors logo(s) for advertising, P.O.S., and merchandising items must be approved through the CO-OP Administration to qualify for funding.

10. Code 3 items (special imprint streamers, banners, etc.) associated with an event will be CO-OPed only after the distributor's Code 3 budget has been exhausted.

11. Funds should not be committed to programs that distributors would support in the absence of such funds. The intent of the CO-OP program is to encourage distributors' supplemental (above and beyond) involvement in their local communities.

12. CO-OP Events will also participate in the following additional activities.
    a. Local trade show
    b. Product/package introduction parties
    c. Free standing hospitality at major sports events excluding transportation, lodging, and tickets for retailers and beer. (A minimum of 10,000 spectators at a sporting event—no fairs, festivals, show, etc.—are necessary to qualify.)

13. The following will not be considered for CO-OP funding:
    a. Beer
    b. Post-offs
    c. Capital equipment
    d. Salaries, bonuses, etc. of Coors distributors' employees
    e. Sales incentive programs
    f. Dinners, banquets, luncheons that are unrelated to an approved CO-OP event, including entertainment at those functions
    g. Gifts/donations (financial or goods)
    h. Purchase of tickets for retailer use by distributors
    i. Transportation or lodging for retailers

REGIONAL EVENTS—Fairs and Festivals

1. For the event to truly be a major regional event, it should draw a significant portion (i.e., 20 percent) of its attendance from outside the host distributor area.
2. Minimum attendance of 200,000 people (or 40,000 per day if it's under a 5-day event).
3. Program cost to Coors of at least $10,000.
4. Distributor participation at a minimum of 30 percent and a maximum of 50 percent of the total cost.
5. Events must receive regional media coverage (media coverage outside the event's metro area).
6. Beer sampling opportunities.
7. Priority states will receive preference (Sales and Brand will define priorities).
8. Non-sporting type events (i.e., fairs, festivals) will receive preference over sporting events (i.e., fights, runs).

REGIONAL EVENTS—Program Development

1. Regional—Program should affect a broad geographic area and population base.
2. Series—Should be multiple number of events executed in different locations conducted either simultaneously or over time.
3. Expandable—Should be able to expand/execute the same program anywhere in Coors market area.
4. High Participation—should be open to "Mass participation," involving large participant and/or spectator numbers.
5. Have Continuity—Program should have potential for multi-year involvement and development by Coors.
6. Contract Executed—Must be organized and executed by a bona fide professional promoter with whom Coors has a signed contract/sponsorship agreement.
7. Distributor Co-Funded—Must be at least 30 percent after the program's first year (T & D) implementation.

SPECIAL MARKETING

Special Marketing will research, evaluate, and develop opportunities that match the young adult's lifestyle and brand objectives. The profile of the young adult target segment applies to both Coors and Coors Light.

1. Demographic profile

Age:	Primary target LDA-24
Segments:	Non-college
	College
Sex:	Primary target: male
	Secondary target: female
Marital status:	Single
Work status:	(Ranked by priority)
	blue collar,
	white collar (gray collar)
	Part-time, unemployed
Ethnic composition:	(Ranked by opportunity)
	Anglo, Hispanic, Black

2. Demographic segmentation (college versus non-college): *

College	Non-college
LDA-26 (same mind set as LDA-24)	LDA-24 (25-29)
Male	Male (primary)
$8-12K year (blue collar influence)	$12-24K year
Single	Single
Anglo	Anglo
White/gray collar	Blue/gray collar

3. Psychographic profile - descriptors characterize college versus non-college young adults

College	Non-college
More likely to consume light beer	Followers
Direction oriented	Subject to heavy peer
More secure	pressure
"Purpose in life"	"World owes me"
Party-women-music	Hedonistic
Somewhat serious minded (focused)	Anti-gay
"Live for today" (smaller degree)	Adventurous
Work hard—play hard	Smaller circle of friends
Self-centered	Macho
Health conscious	Not secure in self
Participant vs. spectator	Work ethic not important
Conservative (see limitations)	Cars important
	"Power symbols"

    *It should be noted that Coors Brand planned to put emphasis on the non-college segment and Coors Light Brand planned to put emphasis on the college segment.

College	Non-college
Not moved by TV imagery	Fantasize/escapism
Not brand loyal	Look for acceptance
Peer pressure (jocks, Greeks, campus leaders)	"Live for today" ethic
Looking for uniqueness in life	Moved by TV imagery
Takes safe choice	Elusive
Into high visibility items that identify self	Party-women-music
	Cynical

4. Activities/recreation:

College	Non-college
Intramural sports	Bar hopping
Parties	Hunting/fishing
Music (concerts, records, tapes)	Motorcycles/motor sports
Movies (high consumption)	Video games
Fraternities (B.M.O.C.)	Music (concerts financially restricted)
Limited transportation	
University sports (spectators)	Movies
Entertainment within close locale	TV-viewing at home (MTV/rock videos)
Photography	
Skiing	Spectator sports (index higher
Playing cards	Y.M.C.A./rec. center oriented
Swimming	
Tennis	
Bowling	Local team participant (i.e. Golf, darts, softball, bowling, basketball).
Weight lifting	
Boating	
Camping	
Jogging	
Racquetball	

Criteria used to select opportunities:

1. Appeal to young adult lifestyle (see previously listed profiles).
2. Uniqueness of events.
3. Activities that can affect large groups of young adults, on a major regional and/or national level.
4. Involve young adult radio (3-to-1 ratio).
5. Entertainment, activities such as music, music-related and comedy.
6. Opportunity for Brand dominance or ownership.
7. Programs that are cost effective and turnkey operative.
8. Activities that are fun and offer an escape from daily pressures.
9. Programs that are extendible through distributor efforts.
10. Cross-promotional opportunities, if applicable.
11. Events that offer consistency and continuity within markets and from market-to-market.
12. Impact in Coors marketing area where high concentrations of young adults reside.
13. Programs that can serve as vehicles for national level/regional advertising and/or consumer promotion opportunities.

References

Castiglione, J. (1989, May). Good neighbors. *College Athletic Management*, pp. 31-33.

Hagstrom, R. (1998). *The NASCAR Way*. New York: Wiley.

IEG (2003, October 20). IEG survey. *IEG Sponsorship Report*, 3-4.

Sherwin-Williams Inks Partnership with Big South (2004). Retrieved February 26 from http://www.sponsorship.com/news/content/5056.asp?source=iotw022604.

Smart brand vehicles to lead runners in the 108th Boston Marathon (2004). Retrieved April 4 from http://sponsorship.com/news/content/5257.asp?source=iotw041504.

Ukman, L. (2004, May 31). Assertions. *IEG Sponsorship Report*, *23* (10), p.2.

Wilkinson, D. G. (1986). *Sport Marketing Institute*. Willowdale, Ontario: Sport Marketing Institute.

Williamson, E. (2004). *Gulf states Toyota*. Retrieved June 7 from http://www.migalareport.com/jun04_story2.cfm.

Sponsor Prospecting Worksheets

The worksheets provide a guide for developing various sections of a sponsorship plan. The following sheets cover potential prospects for sponsorship. Complete these worksheets as a preparatory step in the creation of a sponsorship plan.

Compile a list of all corporations that do business with you.

_____

_____

_____

_____

_____

_____

Identify corporations through various information sources (newspapers, journals) that may have an interest in or connection to sport.

_____

_____

_____

_____

_____

_____

Delineate specific candidates gleaned from your Chamber of Commerce search.

_____

_____

_____

_____

_____

Report specific companies located from a review of the Yellow Page or from drive-by trips through the community.

_____

_____

_____

_____

_____

Specify the most feasible point of contact for each potential sponsor located.

_____

_____

_____

_____

_____

_____

_____

Chapter Three

Identifying Sponsor Needs

Introduction

As noted in Chapter 1, sponsorship in sport has been predicated on exchange theory with benefits accruing to sponsors and sport organizations alike. This chapter addresses the needs of the corporation. A quintessential need for any corporation is to differentiate itself from its competitors via a competitive advantage. A successful sport sponsorship may be an effective mechanism in creating and sustaining that advantage (Amis, Pant, & Slack, 1997).

Sponsor Rationale

According to AT&T's vice president of advertising and communication, "It's no longer a world where company CEOs decide to sponsor their favorite sports at any cost. Sponsorships are business decisions that must go through the same profit and loss assessment as any other" (Graham, 1998, p. 34). This point was further reinforced by the Michael Payne, former IOC Marketing Director, who said "Corporation bosses are increasingly having to justify their marketing investments to their shareholders and can no longer just say being associated with the Olympics is good for a company—they will have to prove it with hard facts" (Keeping the Olympics, 1997, p. 32). Perhaps the best clarification of what sponsors are looking for in their relationships with sport organizations was forwarded by Lopiano (cited in Reynolds, 1998, p. 30): "Sponsorships have to measure up on a performance basis in their ability to match the right demographic and psychographic targets, reach the appropriate decision makers and ultimately help move product or services."

Corporate Criteria for Sponsor Evaluation

According to Ukman (2004a, p. vii), "talk to any four sponsors of any property and you will find that while they are sponsoring the same property, each is using sponsorship to accomplish different objectives." For example, banks may be interested in new customer acquisition and business-to-business (B-2-B) relationships, while automotive sponsors may be looking to showcase new models and drive floor traffic. The criteria used by sponsors in their evaluation of proposals have been discussed extensively in the literature. Many corporations have developed definitive criteria, while others are more subjective.

Perhaps the most comprehensive study of corporate criteria was Irwin, Assimakopoulos, and Sutton's (1994). Their initial foray into sponsorship research produced a model for use by corporations in the evaluation of sponsorship proposals. Their model presented an array of factors, which corporations could assess in a comparative fashion, for all proposals received. These factors (Irwin, Assimakopoulos, & Sutton, 1994, p. 59):

Budget considerations	Event management
Affordability	Event profile
Tax benefits	Organizing committee
Position/image	Media guarantees
Product-sport image fit	Legal status
Product utility fit	Governing body status
Image-target fit	Marketing agency profile
Targeting of market	Integrated communications
Extended media coverage	Extended audience

Immediate audience	Public relations/publicity
Competition consideration	Sales promotions
Competition's interest	Personal selling
Ambush market avoidance	Strategies
Level of involvement	Type of sponsorship
Title sponsor	Established
Major sponsor	New
Co-sponsor	Team
In-kind sponsor	League/championship
Exclusivity	Event
Long-term involvement	Facility
Once-off	

Further research was conducted to test the validity of their model. They found that the factors rated as most important were *fit between sport image and product/service image, target market fit, demographic profile of the extended audience, demographic fit of the immediate audience,* and *opportunities for signage* (Irwin, Assimakopoulos, & Sutton, 1994). Additional research by Thwaites and Aguilar-Manjarrez (1997) found that community involvement and enhancement of the company image were also highly rated. Their study also found that corporate hospitality and building trade relations were considered as important factors for companies seeking sport sponsorships. However, a considerable amount of research has shown that market-driven objectives such as *increased market share, new client acquisition, new product awareness,* and *on-site sales* have been cited as critical factors (Copeland, Frisby, & McCarville, 1996; Irwin & Sutton, 1994; Kuzma, Shanklin & McCally, 1993). Stotlar's (1999) research and Seaver's (2004) study of 50 leading US sport sponsors revealed that sales and market-specific objectives were considered the most critical components in a sponsorship partnership. Those items that corporate executives rated most highly were the ability to a) create new customers, b) quantifiably increase sales, and c) tie-in to current marketing strategy. Ukman (2004a) identified the top five sponsorship objectives as *increasing brand loyalty, increasing awareness, change/reinforce image, drive retail sales,* and *stimulate product trial.* Obviously, there is considerable agreement across the industry. Several industry-based examples are illustrated below.

Among the sponsorship elements that Reebok expects in its event sponsorships are *on-site and local retailer sales activities, product expos and new product sampling, promotions of their national account representatives,* Reebok athlete clinics and autograph sessions, scheduled press receptions, course signage and banners, national network coverage and hospitality/VIP accommodations (Rohm, 1997). Volvo, a long-time sport sponsor, forwarded additional thoughts regarding for their sponsorship decisions. Through their ups and downs with tennis, they felt that a company should make large rather than small investments. "The big investment gives much more brand name exposure and at the same time, is relatively less work" (Volvo and Sport Sponsorship, 1990, p. 5). Their philosophy also indicated a long-term commitment for 5-10 years was more beneficial.

One of the basic criteria involved in matching sport organizations with sponsors is to establish a demographic fit between the sport organization's participant/audience base and the target market of the sponsor. For instance, the outboard engine manufacturer Evinrude sponsors several fishing tournaments. Their VP of sales and marketing said "we are able to have a presence in front of enthusiastic anglers nearly year-round, and anglers are one of our most important markets" ("Evinrude renews," 2004).

Economic factors are also a key element in a sponsor-event match. Investment firm Charles Schwab signed on to sponsor the PGA Tour through 2008. Not only can Schwab entertain high-income clients through their hospitality program, but they also provide investment-related services to PGA players and staff. The match seems better than if they were to sponsor action sports where fans and participants typically have less discretionary funds to invest. Companies sponsoring action sports are often looking to capture the elusive young consumer in order to influence life-long brand loyalty. Age represents one of the demographic variables in which sponsors may be interested, but gender may surface as another critical factor. While some corporations focus on a predominately male demographic, "companies are waking up to the power of marketing to women" (Reynolds, 1998, p. 30). Selecting the right fit with the sponsor on this variable is equally important.

When addressing demographics, the sport marketer should be sure to elaborate about how a sponsor can benefit from this component. For example, convincing a sponsor that the demographic composition of an event is a good match with the corporation's target market is only the first step. The sport marketer can make their database available for the sponsor's use in direct mail marketing. The National Athletic Trainers Association allows sponsors to access its 20,000 bi-monthly emails, noting, "if sponsors want to get a message out, we want them to use every communications piece we have available" ("Five Key Factors," 2004, p. 3). When AT&T Wireless, Sunkist and Ace Hardware sponsored Little League Baseball, not only did they get signage at tournaments and other promotional elements, they got access to Little League Baseball's database (Lefton, 2003). This allowed sponsoring corporations to mail advertising messages directly to 3 million Little League players.

There has, however, been an outcry that these actions result in an over-commercialization of youth sport. In an effort to reduce such protests, the American Youth Soccer Organization performs direct mailing for sponsors, so that AYSO can screen any offensive material (Johnson, 1998; Dunn, 2004). Although access to a sport organization's database may make a proposal more enticing, perhaps the most ethical practice may be to limit the use of mailing lists by sponsors to adult constituents and, then, include only those who have consented.

Understanding and affecting consumer psychographics—the attitudes, beliefs, and feelings of consumers—is also important to companies engaged in sponsorship. In this light, The US Army has been very active in a variety of racing programs. They sponsor vehicles in both the NHRA and NASCAR. The psychographic profile of those fans, and the ability to set up displays with Hummers, tanks and a climbing wall further enhance their ability to attract new recruits. Another interesting match is handgun maker Smith & Wesson's decision to sponsor a NASCAR team and driver. Loyalty patterns are also extremely important to sponsors. "Data say that about 73% of NASCAR fans choose the products of their sport's sponsors over others" (King, 1998, p. 9). In 2004, data showed that NASCAR fans were three times more likely to purchase a sponsor's product over a similar product from a non-sponsor (Drehs, 2004). Pitts (2003) also found high consumer loyalty in her study of Gay Games sponsors, determining that 68% of participants recognized sponsors and 74% of attendees intended to purchase from sponsors. The gay and lesbian market represents a $22 billion sport market.

As one author noted, "It is theoretically possible to put up the money to sponsor an event, hang a big billboard at the event, and have that be the end of it. But any organization that looked on sponsorship in this limited fashion would be foolish indeed" (Hagstrom, 1998, p. 51). Thus, sponsors can avail themselves of an array of benefits attainable through sport sponsorship. To complement the research findings in this area, additional cases are presented highlighting corporate objectives in commonly cited categories: awareness, image, sales, hospitality, and employee motivation.

Awareness Objectives

Understanding sponsor rationale regarding awareness has a lot to do with television. Ehrlich (1998) posed the question, "What do the 20 official sponsors and suppliers of the World Cup hope to get from their involvement? Not just exposure in front of 2.5 million ticket holders. . . .They're after a piece of the 36 billion cumulative television audience" (p. 26). An important aspect of sport sponsorship that cannot be overlooked for the coming decade is the aspect of globalization. In a world economy, companies may find it difficult to communicate to consumers in Zimbabwe or China, but a sport sponsorship can help cut through some of the existing barriers. For example, UPS, a worldwide sponsor of the Olympic Games, viewed its sponsorship of the 2000 Olympics as an opportunity to make new international business contacts and hoped to reap benefits from these contacts in future business dealings (Kennet, Sneath, & Erdmann, 1998).

The awareness objective can be effective if relatively few consumers know anything about the sponsor's product or company. However, it has been shown to do little for a company like Coca-Cola. John Cordova (1996), senior business manager for Coca-Cola, referred to event signage as "wallpaper." In the 1980s, Coke's advertising motto was "if it stands still paint it red, if it moves, sponsor it." This "be everywhere" strategy has been replaced by "consumer activation." In addition, their internal research showed that stadium signage did not drive product sales. Coke found that there was not enough profit from in-stadium product sales to justify large sponsorship expenditures. Furthermore, even "pouring rights" in the stadium were of marginal value. Coke found that the ridiculously high prices charged by some sport concessionaires were being blamed on Coke (Cordova, 1996). A similar note was sounded by Miller Brewing Company's director of sport marketing when he said, "the strategy is much more than how much signage we get. Visibility is not the key for us. Everyone knows who Miller is, but we need inventory that makes the brand come alive" (Lauletta, 2003, p. 8).

Additional support concerning the tenuous value of awareness came from former Nike marketing Vice President, Steve Miller, when he indicated that Nike did not factor exposure of their logo into sponsorship valuation. He believed that if people didn't recognize a Swoosh before the sponsorship, they never would. With college sponsorships, Nike has been more interested in how much product the partnership could sell at retail. This was the under pinning of Nike's agreement with the University of Michigan, the number one selling licensed collegiate brand. When Nike secured sponsorship of sport programs at the United States Air Force Academy (USAFA), it is not that Nike was uninterested in the TV exposure garnered through the Air Force football team's televised games and Bowl appearances, but they are more attracted to the $5 million a year in merchandise sales through the USAFA visitor's center, 33% of which was Nike product. In summary, sport marketing executives Amshay and Brian (1998) summarized the issue in stating, "exposure has value, but it is hugely overrated" (p. 23).

Image Objectives

A company's image is the sum of beliefs, ideas, and impressions held by consumers about the company and its products (Ries & Trout, 1986). Given this concept, research has shown that sport sponsorship can help shape an otherwise obscure corporate image, but it can do little to change one. This was exemplified when Kmart Corporation attempted sponsorship of various PGA golf events to try to elevate their image by tying it to an upscale event. The strategy was not, however, very successful.

This component can be observed in a variety of settings. Rolex does not sponsor rodeo events and Copenhagen Chewing Tobacco does not sponsor yachting. McDonald's (1998) research supported the benefits of matching the image of the sport with the image of the corporation. His research confirmed that a sponsorship was more effective if there was a high level of congruence between the image of the sport and that of the company. The concepts around which he evaluated perceptual fit included the terms "Sophisticated," "Rugged," "Exciting," and "Wholesome." His research concluded that the creation a good perceptual fit between the sport event and the sponsoring company could contribute to brand equity for the sponsor (McDonald, 1998).

An excellent overview of the sponsorship of the New Zealand Rugby Union's All Blacks by adidas is provided by, Motion, S. Leitch, and R. Brodie (2003; see additional readings). Following the scheme forwarded above by McDonald, the key attributes of the All Blacks were determined to be "power," "masculinity," "commitment," "teamwork," "New Zealand," "tradition," and "inspirational" (Motion et. al., 2003, 1087). "When adidas evaluates a potential partner they look for two or three matching brand values present in their make-up or in the style in which they take part in sport." The values of 'tradition' and 'New Zealand' were matched to the adidas value of 'authentic'" (Motion et al., 2003, p. 1087). The authors summarized that "adidas and the All Blacks brand values were compatible and connected at a fundamental level" (Motion et al., 2003, p. 1090).

Sales Objectives

Sales objectives include such factors as increasing the sales levels of certain brands and getting people to sample a product. In most of the recent research on corporate criteria, the sales factor ranks near the top of the list of important considerations for corporations looking to engage in sport sponsorship (Stotlar, 1999). Steve Saunders (1996), marketing Vice President at Coors, said that the bottom line for a Coors sport sponsorship is always, "Does it sell beer?" To illustrate the point, consider the case of Coors' association with the Colorado Rockies baseball team. At Coors Field, Coors has a microbrewery from which it bottles and sells specialty beer in the stadium and the general market. It also sells a significant volume of beer during the 81 home games and other events at Coors Field. Within the same industry Anheuser-Busch VP for Sport Marketing Tony Ponturo (2002) said, "It's not our goal to be a sponsor, our goal is to sell our product."

In assessing the value of Coors involvement, Saunders (1996) added that the days of "playing calculus" are over. His reference to calculus was that in previous years, Coors has utilized a formula calculating a summative value of X dollars for a stadium sign, X dollars for pouring rights, X dollars per impression (they actually used $.05 per spectator), and X dollars for title to the event. In Saunders's view, corporate valuation beyond the 1990s will be based on the ability of an event to sell beer on-site, increase market share and to provide direct product profits through Coors distributors.

For many companies engaged in retail sales, floor traffic equates to increased sales. Therefore, in a very successful arrangement with Wendy's restaurants, the United States Association for Blind Athletes (USABA) created the SportMates program. Through this sponsorship, Wendy's would make a donation to USABA for each designated combo meal sold. This promotion resulted in a one-month sales increase of 34.5% for Colorado Wendy's outlets and raised $25,000 for the USABA. In another case, Mercedes-Benz sponsored one of the top professional tennis tournaments (ATP) and was able to sell over 150 cars to tournament players alone. They also offered promotions in tournament host cities to create floor traffic and test drives. These combinations have proven very successful for Mercedes.

Adidas signed up with the Royal & Ancient Golf Course in St. Andrews Scotland as their official supplier. Not only does adidas outfit all of the staff during their gold tournaments, but it also has exclusive sales of gold apparel from the pro shop. Although the numbers are not available, it can be assumed that a large portion of visitors to the birthplace of golf would take home a golf shirt as a souvenir.

Product sampling has also been an effective sponsorship tool, assisting sponsors in attracting potential consumers. U.S. Swimming and Johnson & Johnson's Sundown Sunscreen products implemented one such example. Their sponsorship agreement provided that Johnson & Johnson send sample packets of sunscreen to over 2000 local swim clubs for distribution at area swim meets. This met one of the primary objectives of the company, to get the product into the hands of the most likely customers. Who better than young swimmers and their families?

Product sampling continually generates a great deal of interest in the product and sales can be tracked to indicate an overall effect on sales. It also has been shown to be effective in developing consumer loyalty and providing the company with reliable feedback on products with minimal costs.

Service companies can also generate sales through sport sponsorship. The New England's (insurance and investments) involvement focused on tennis' AT&T Challenge stop on the ATP Tour. The results from their $50,000 sponsorship of the event generated 2,500 leads and over $200,000 in insurance sold. Here, sponsorship strategies centered on effective sales objectives as the primary criterion. In addition, another sport executive also commented that the "focus should not be strictly on exposure, but [be] more sales driven" (Seaver, 1996, p. 33). According to a recent industry survey, a sponsor was quoted as saying "It's real simple. Ultimately, what we have to do is to sell product. A banner ad does not cut it. We need to know that our involvement sold something" (Seaver, 2004, p. 17). One director of sponsorships said, "we are no longer satisfied with enhanced image; give us opportunities for on-site sales. . . dealer tie-ins and we'll listen" (Seaver, 1996, p. 34).

Thus, the relationship between sport organizers and sponsors has evolved accentuating "return on investment" (ROI). The manager of IBM's Olympic sponsorship program commented, "It's not philanthropic; it's not corporate contribution money. The goal is to help gain market share" (Sponsors reveal, 1997, p. 5). Irwin and Sutton's (1994) research on corporate criteria found that market-driven objectives such as increasing sales and market share were highly rated as criterion in sponsorship selection. Calculated value assessment replaced other factors as the primary strategy employed by both event owners and sponsors during the 1990s.

In support of this transition, the top-ranked criterion in Seaver's (2004) industry survey was "a program with the ability to drive quantifiable sales into area retailers" (76% ranked it as extremely important and 20% cited it as important). Xerox personified this concept in their Olympic sponsorship campaigns. They carefully tracked their sales records that revealed 35,000 leads and the sale of more than 6000 copiers directly attributable to their Olympic strategy and marketing initiatives (Stotlar, 1997).

Reebok has also emphasized the sales aspect when it evaluates road-race sponsorships. They prioritize events where they can sell product at the race site or, alternatively, involve local Reebok retailers. In another example, the CEO of Ranger Fishing Boats, sponsor of several bass fishing tournaments, said sponsorship is not about delivering a million impressions, but about getting the message to someone who is going to buy a $20,000 boat in the next 12 months. The clear message is that helping a sponsor move product can develop deeper revenue. Coca-Cola's Cordova said, "bring me a promotion that will put a Coke in the hands of a 12 year old and we can work a deal" (Cordova, 1996).

Both Coca-Cola and Pepsi have consummated countless sponsorship arrangements with public school districts, private schools and colleges and universities across the country. In their association with Jefferson County School District in Colorado, Pepsi procured signage in 59 schools and on 10 school buses in addition to exclusive vending rights on school property. In return, each high school received $25,000; junior high schools were given $15,000 while the elementary schools made $3,000 apiece. While some members of the community were opposed to what they saw as an over-commercialization of schools, the majority of citizens supported the sponsorship.

Hospitality Objectives

Sponsors need places and events to use for entertaining potential clients and enhancing business-to-business relationships (B-2-B). Sporting events have, for many years, provided great opportunities for this activity. NASCAR has been one of the more successful sports in leveraging its popularity through hospitality activities. First, all of the racetracks offer corporate suites in conjunction with sponsorship packages. At Darlington International Raceway, the suites have been priced at $200,000 and have attracted companies like Interstate Batteries, Pepsi, and DuPont. DuPont, which sponsors Jeff Gordon's racecar, typically entertains up to 2,000 clients, employees and associates at a single event, taking them on tours of the pits, providing them a fabulous meal and letting them visit with Jeff Gordon prior to moving up to their suite to watch the race. At the Colonial golf tournament, sponsor Bank of America brought in 1,000 of its top clients to its 13th hole skybox and invited 40 VIPs (so-called "high value" clients) to extend their stay and play the course the day after the tournament. Similar tactics were in place at the America's Cup sailing races, where some sponsors hired yachts to cruise the racecourse while conducting hospitality events. Hospitality does not come cheap. At the 2005 US Open (Golf) at Pinehurst, a tent in the sponsor village started at $100,000 for 50 guests and went to $750,000 for a more sophisticated clubhouse location. These prices typically do not include any food and beverage service, just the space to entertain.

Hospitably is often referred to as business-to-business marketing. This is where businesses can develop relationships with their best customers. It's about influence and what the industry refers to as creating a "network" position. Compaq Computers uses their sponsorships to develop relationships and influence information technology (IT) decision makers in the nation's leading companies. According to Ethan Green, former sponsorship manager at Compaq, among the company's sponsorship criteria was the involvement of IT decision makers with the event. The company was less interested in influencing consumers purchasing low-end computers every few years than they were in targeting people who would make the decision to purchase computers, networks, and printers for major corporations (Green, 2002). In 2003, when Bank of America signed on as sponsor of the Colonial Golf Tournament, it wanted to improve the bank's relationships with its key accounts. They created "Hogan's Alley," resembling a fine country club with conversation areas, food, and entertainment. Their research after the event showed that 73% of attendees thought it was the best corporate hospitality that they had ever experienced. More importantly, 84% said that the experience strengthened their relationship with the bank. FedEx uses its relationship with the NFL to provide hospitality events in stadiums on non-game days. These events provide controlled sales environments that capitalize on the draw of the team. They also give FedEx an experience that the typical fan cannot buy. "Hospitality is sponsorship and marketing at its best because it allows a company to achieve so many objectives" (Migala, 2004a).

Employee Morale Objectives

One established method of increasing employee morale is to involve famous athletes in corporate affairs. Texaco has a longstanding association with racing's Mario Andretti and has used him as a motivational speaker in numerous corporate meetings. After his speech, Andretti would sign autographs and mingle with employees and discuss the importance of hard work and attention to detail. Similarly, Xerox used 1996 decathlon gold medalist Dan O'Brien for corporate presentations prior to the Atlanta Games. Not only did this activity inspire employees at work, but it also gave them an incentive to watch the games and cheer for O'Brien.

VISA has also successfully used its Olympic sponsorship to build team spirit within the corporation. One of its techniques was to make Olympic logo golf shirts available to all employees. During the lead up to the Games, they had to re-order shirts five different times because of the high demand. Another Olympic Games sponsorship example occurred when John Hancock Insurance utilized its worldwide sponsorship of the Olympic Games to motivate their employees. Their sales staff responded to opportunities to win expense-paid trips to the Atlanta Olympic Games and the company realized revenue increases of 50% in 1995 and 35% in 1996 (Kennet, Sneath and Erdmann, 1998).

Other Sponsor Objectives

Other criteria upon which companies make sponsorship decisions include other current sponsors and mix of products; corporate relations with other sponsors; co-operation from the host facility for signage, access, and placement; and the potential for VIP contacts. An outline of the sponsorship needs examined by Anheuser-Busch is presented in Figure 3-1.

The number of events and their geographic representation are also key elements in sponsor decisions. The International Events Group has clarified the difference between national and regional events. Ukman (2004b) indicated that to be considered a "national" event, the sponsorship impact would need to affect 15 major markets. Otherwise, it should be classified as a regional event. Major companies that have national or international distribution channels are always interested in wholesaler tie-ins. This typically relates to the ability of a local distributor to have special promotions, on-site displays, and possibly cooperative advertising. Some corporations are also drawn to sport sponsorship by the potential for merchandising. Miller Brewing Company began selling facsimile jackets and T-shirts on the NASCAR auto racing circuit and not only realized substantial profits from the products themselves, but increased its visibility and extended its influence into the local community for periods far in excess of the race day. UPS generated over $500 million dollars in sales of branded merchandise in the first month of its sponsorship of Dale Jarrett's NASCAR team.

Activation

The power of relevant activation cannot be overlooked. Sponsors need to communicate with each of the audiences in meaningful ways. Throwing up a sign and putting the sponsor's logo in the game program won't work. Coca-Cola uses its sponsorship of the Olympic Games to extend their reach into the community by also sponsoring the Olympic Torch Relay. Involvement of local Coke bottlers in the nomination process for torch runners brings their involvement into each community. In 2004, the first time the torch traveled internationally, Coke activated their sponsorship across China, Africa and throughout the international route of the torch. Coke used another activation strategy when it took over sponsorship of the National Hot Rod Association (NHRA) with its PowerAde brand. As title sponsor, Coke wanted to connect with racing fans. It launched a special flavor of their sport drink called NHRA PowerAde after field testing and online research with NHRA fans.

Figure 3.1
Anheuser-Busch
Sports Sponsorship Evaluation

Season Tickets
a. Complimentary
b. Discount
c. Full Purchase Availability

Reserved Seat Tickets
a. Complimentary
b. Discount
c. Full Purchase Availability

Use of On-Air Talent
a. Lead-ins
b. Drop-in
c. Live Announcer
d. Special Promo Sports
e. No Charge
f. Charge (amount)
g. Re-use Off Station
    On Camera
    Off Camera

General Admission Tickets
a. Complimentary
b. Discount
c. Full Purchase Availability
d. Blocks for Charity Use
e. Scoreboard Mention
f. Invitations

Special Stadium Nights
a. Free Tickets
b. Special Meeting Room
c. Souvenirs/Programs
d. First-Ball Ceremony

Yearbook/Press Guide Ads
a. Complimentary
b. Discount
c. Full Purchase
d. Number of Complimentary Copies

Arena Signage
a. Availability
b. Number
c. Included
d. Extra Charge (amount)

Program Ads
a. Complimentary
b. Discount Purchase
c. Full Purchase
d. Number of Complimentary Copies

Special Items
a. Use of VIP Rooms
b. Use of Luxury Box
c. League/Press Passes
d. Parking Passes
e. Ticket Purchase Option
f. Use of Highlight Film
g. Use of Product Music
h. Merchandising
i. Sampling Opportunity

Scoreboard/PA Exposure in Stadium
a. Complimentary
b. Discount
c. Full Purchase
d. Number and Frequency

Participation in Events
a. Pre-Game
b. Half Time
c. On-Field or On-Floor
d. Awards Presentations

In another Olympic-related sponsorship VISA was able to activate its card usage through member banks by offering sweepstakes for trips to the games. At one bank the sweepstakes, where every transaction with a VISA card qualified as an entry into the drawing, bank revenues increased 300% over a control group during the 60-day promotion (Staying ahead of the Games, 2004). At Turner field in Atlanta, sponsorship with the area Lexus dealers provides reserved parking for Lexus owners. BMW also activated its sponsorship with American Ski Corporation (owner of seven ski resorts) by supplying BMW sport utility vehicles as a courtesy for hotel guests. The program generated 15,000 test drives. At the higher levels, BMW invited 150 of its bests customers for expense-paid ski vacations. This brings the customer directly in touch with the benefits of the sponsorship.

Industry data showed that a lot of sponsors are not spending enough money on activation. Performance Research (2004) found that 70% of sponsors are spending less than the suggested $3-to-$1 on activation. The industry average in 2003 was only $1.75 for each dollar spent. MasterCard Vice President of Global Sponsorships and Event Marketing, Bob Cramer commented,

> We are talking about activation with more and more of our partners. We are looking at activation like inventory, and properties need to do the same. It is hard pill for properties to swallow because it is not so much about what they can do for us at the event but in the marketplace (Migala, 2004).

Activation also encompasses using the sponsorship across the business. This is often referred to as *integration*. Cordiner (2002, p. 15) noted that "brands need to integrate sponsorship across all business activity to make it work, and the relationship between brand and sports property needs to be nurtured and developed over time to be truly effective." An example of integration was seen in Saturn's sponsorship of Arizona State University's 2003 homecoming activities. Not only did Saturn get vehicle displays and hospitality sites at all of the athletic events, but it received ID in football broadcasts and on 125,00 direct mail pieces that went out to students and alumni ("University reaps," 2003). Another example of corporate integration on sponsorship activities can be seen with the FedEx example in the Best Practice section of this chapter.

Another emerging activation follows the marketing trend of *experience marketing*. Through sponsorship corporations are looking for ways to relate to their products and enhance their experience with the event. "Sponsors will look for an individual, event, club or organization in the sports arena that carries a sufficiently high level of emotional involvement with their target audience" (Cordiner, 2002, p. 14). Furthermore, "sponsorship must motivate consumers to interact with the sponsor's product—whether that's touching it, using it, speaking to a specialist about it, etc.—and have them walk away with more knowledge about it" (Product integration, 2004, p. 3). Green (2002) identified integration as one of Compaq's key elements in sponsorship screening. If the sport property does not integrate Compaq Computers into the event, they are not interested. Thus the Houston Marathon was able to secure Compaq as a sponsor by using computers to track runners on the course both from the sponsor's on-site tent and through their web site. These experiences will, in turn, increase consumer purchase intentions. While including these types of elements creates added benefits, the situation should not be left to chance. The extent and level of integration should be formalized in the contract, noting the specific activities that will ensure success.

An excellent example of integration occurred in Nextel's sponsorship of NASCAR. Nextel created FanScan In-car Audio, a wireless service that connects fans with the live communications between drivers and their pits during the race. "Nextel's affiliation with NASCAR is based entirely on how we can leverage our core competencies in wireless communication to enhance the fan experience . . . immersing them in the entire experience so that they are part of the action" ("Nextel launches," 2004).

Cross-Promotion

Cross promotion, the ability of sponsors to work cooperatively in a sponsorship, has been noted as "among the most powerful and popular activation methods, as they can grant marketers access to new distribution channels and spread out promotional costs across multiple partners" ("Five Key Factors," 2004, p.3). The NHL Phoenix Coyotes put together a deal with the team, Coke, and Fry's Grocery. Fry's, a primary Coyotes sponsor, offered the team control of the store entry end-caps (the end section of each of shopping isle) in each store as part of their sponsorship. Coke desperately wanted end-cap control to lure consumers to their product, so the team arranged a trade with tickets and special Coke cans from Fry's wherein kids received a free ticket with each adult ticket purchased. The cross-promotion produced increased floor traffic for Fry's, incremental sales for Coke, and sold Coyotes tickets. Coke cross-promotes its NASCAR sponsorship by partnering with primary sponsor Home Depot stores by featuring Home Depot Team driver on its Coke machines at all stores.

The Coyotes also secured a cross-promotion arrangement with Budweiser. This deal provided for 18 Budweiser semi-trailer trucks to be outfitted with Coyotes' murals on the side. In covering their distribution routes, these trucks drove all over Arizona and New Mexico promoting the Coyotes hockey team 24 hours per day.

Another successful match was made in a cross-promotion opportunity between Kellogg and NASCAR. As a sponsor of an individual racecar, Kellogg was able to develop nation-wide promotions utilizing the NASCAR brand and giveaway miniature cars in its cereal boxes. "Our objective is to leverage the popularity of stock car racing so we can drive incremental volume" (Goldberg, 1998a, p. 22). Many NASCAR sponsors have found tremendous success with retail tie-ins through "show car" programs. Facsimile racecars are transported around the country in association with area retailers to promote the company's involvement in racing. These events consistently draw large crowds and ultimately move a lot of product off store shelves. In the sport of fishing, sponsors of a series of fishing tournaments banded together to package their products for participants and spectators that included Evinrude out-board motors, Ranger fishing boats and Ever-Start Marine Batteries in the "Ultimate Fishing Package" ("Evinrude renews," 2004). In another cross promotion, Olympic partner Coca-Cola persuaded one of the athletes it sponsors, 2004 Olympic wrestler Shane Hamman, to spend a day at fellow sponsor 24 Hour Fitness working out with a lucky employee and gym member who won an in-store contest. As part of the contest, 24 Hour Fitness, in turn, promoted Coca-Cola's PowerAde line of sports drinks.

Sponsors are also motivated by the type and amount of press coverage, both print and electronic, that they receive as a result of the sponsorship. Sport organizations can utilize data collected from previous events (or from similar events if a new event is proposed) to convince sponsors there is a sufficient media value returned through the sponsorship program. The data could include column inches that appeared in the newspaper and airtime of news or special reports related to the event on television and radio.

The timing of an event can also play an important role in sport sponsorship. Companies continually introduce new products and services to the market. A growing number of cruise lines are using sport sponsorship to promote new cruise activities like climbing walls and adventure side-trips. Airlines are adding new cities to their routes and tying an event into a new destination can prove advantageous for the airline. In addition, seasonal timing should be examined as well. Automobile dealers typically introduce the new model year in the fall. This could be a perfect match to the football season where the new products could be displayed at games. In another example, EAS computer game maker has sponsored the Maui Invitational basketball tournament. This tournament has featured the nation's top collegiate teams and falls at the beginning of the holiday shopping season in late November. Circumstances like these create enormous opportunities for sport marketers as the new companies were looking for effective strategies to promote their new identity.

Details surrounding an event's organizing committee are also important to potential sponsors. The event organizers should be well prepared and financially stable with a proven record with other activities. Sponsors are always going to be cautious about lending their name and corporate identity to another entity. Therefore, attention to stability and professionalism is imperative.

Sponsors are also wary of the multitude of risks that may be associated with an event. The potential for a public relations disaster should be tolerable. There are always risks, some dealing with the weather, but the organizers should be willing to point out potential risks to the sponsor. One recent example illustrates the point. When Dodge trucks became involved in the sponsorship of a major sled dog race (Iditarod), they were unaware that the public relations generated from animal rights activists could produce a substantial amount of negative press coverage and controversy. Similar risks can be found with rodeo events. As a preemptive maneuver to offset such a controversy, the Professional Rodeo Cowboys Association published a brochure on the protections and humane treatment of animals that sponsors can use to explain the activities and defend their events.

Sometimes even the type of sponsorship can cause controversy. In 2004, the Daytona Cubs (Triple A baseball team) conducted a funeral giveaway to the best essay on a fan's ideal funeral. The program was sponsored by a local funeral home but caused many in the community to be upset over what they considered to be the trivialization of death ("Baseball's Cubs run free funeral promotion," 2004)

Cause-Related Sponsorship

One of the most significant trends in sport marketing is to affiliate a sport sponsorship with a popular cause. Muellner (1998) noted, "Without a doubt, there are a lot more companies trying to market with cause-related endeavors" (p. 8). The rationale for involvement in cause-related marketing is clear when a more detailed look at consumer response is considered. Irwin, Lackowitz, Cornwell, and Clark (2003, p. 138) noted that "it is critical that the CRM [cause-related marketing] tie-in be viewed a valuable and genuine to the consumer. They noted that 83% of consumers developed a more positive impression of companies engaged in CRM. Several examples of this practice can be detected throughout the sport industry (also refer to Chapter 1).

In 1996, an event was developed to honor the late college basketball coach Jim Valvano and raise money for cancer research. The college basketball tournament entitled "Coaches vs. Cancer" raises over $1,000,000 each year. Another example is the Terry Fox Run to raise funds to fight cancer, which began in 1995. This event has been held in 53 countries and has been one of the most ambitious international cause-related sporting events. Furthermore, Race for the Cure represents another very popular running event held annually in numerous communities across the US to raise money for breast cancer research. Since its inception, Race for the Cure has raised over $50 million, the majority of which stays in the host communities. An example of retailer involvement in cause-related marketing was seen when Rykä shoes and Lady Foot Locker joined together to contribute of 1% of purchases to the Another Chance Foundation. A detailed review of their program is shown in Figure 3-2.

Figure 3.2
Another Chance Foundation
Rykä - Lady Foot Locker

Another Chance Foundation's mission is to support programs that encourage women in need to attain greater self-sufficiency and make health and fitness integral parts of their lives. Rykä believes in encouraging and educating all women in their quest to be fit and active and created Another Chance with the goal of "Helping Women Get on Their Feet."

As founding sponsors of Another Chance Foundation, Rykä and Lady Foot Locker have formed a partnership that provides a great opportunity to give back and make a difference in many women's lives. Another Chance Foundation will distribute funds to organizations that support programs for women that encourage greater self-sufficiency through a healthy and fit lifestyle.

One percent (1%) of all retail sales of Rykä product sold at Lady Foot Locker will be donated to Another Chance Foundation.

Another Chance Foundation will also seek additional contributions from corporations and like-minded organizations that share the same goals and ideals for women's lives.

According to Rykaä President Mary Taylor, "Rykä is returning to its roots and the philosophy forged by the brand's founder, Sheri Poe. Rykä is committed to encouraging and educating in their quest to be fit and active, and Another Chance will enable women who need assistance with this goal to achieve it."

Another Chance Foundation
10 Mount Vernon Street
PMB #231
Winchester, MA 01890

"Studies support the notion that consumers feel better about a brand they believe is contributing to society" (Muellner, 1998, p. 8). In 2004 an IEG sponsorship report (Ukman, 2004c, p. 2) indicated, "Nearly half of Americans are engaged in some form of consumer activation" making buying decisions on the social actions of the companies from which they purchase products. Furthermore, "the more affluent the consumer, as well as the more highly-educated, the more they participated in consumer activism." Their research also showed that 78% of consumers would buy from a sponsoring company that was associated with a worthy cause about which they cared. In addition, 66% reported they would switch brands, 62% would switch retailers, and 54% said they would pay more (5-10%) for items offered by a company that was involved with an important cause (Ukman, 1997, p. 2). Consumers were equally perturbed at companies that lacked a viable philanthropy program. More than 50% of consumers had actually boycotted products from companies that were not active in social programs. Despite all of the success, some degree of caution must be exercised in cause-related marketing campaigns. One marketing executive noted, "If something is done purely for publicity, people see through it . . .It has to come from a motivation to work for the betterment of the community" (Muellner, 1998, p. 8)

Grassroots (Community-Based) Sponsorship

Grassroots sponsorship brings marketing to a local community or region as opposed to a national scope. Pepsi modified its strategy for multicultural sport marketing in 2004 opting to spread their dollars across a greater number of small events with focused ethnic profiles ("Pepsi wants," 2004). Previous research has shown that several factors evident in national sponsorship selection were the same as those for sponsoring grassroots sport, most notably, increasing corporate exposure and consumer awareness. Another advantage of grassroots sport sponsorship includes increased availability for product sampling and prototype testing as additional ways to reach consumers. The authors noted that in grassroots sport sponsorship "corporations are increasingly pumping money into grassroots sports organizations, and in turn, grassroots sports organizations are better able to provide corporations with substantial returns on their investments (Greenwald & Fernandez-Balboa, 1998, p. 42). These companies are realizing that speaking to consumers in a local environment may be more persuasive than through nationwide involvement.

One of the issues surrounding grassroots sport sponsorship is related to the professionalism of the local organization. This concern seems logical because national corporations tend to be less secure about putting their brand image in the hands of volunteers or unproven local organizers than they would be with major sport organizations or professional leagues. One industry executive commented, "There are just too many bad events. An event might have a couple of thousand kids, but not the media and PR. You pay a guy a couple of thousand dollars to support an event and you never know what happened" (Joyce, 2003, p. 8).

The quest for sponsors can be an exciting and rewarding one, but be assured that the sport marketer must consider the needs and objectives of the sponsor. The Marketing Director for Anaheim Sports cautioned sport administrators that sponsor relationships can evolve into ones where the sponsors desire more for their money than has previously been delivered. He said, "We can't just put their sign up, but must figure out how to drive traffic in their store or service" (Goldberg, 1998b). The collective criteria used by sponsors to evaluate sponsorship opportunities do not seem to vary considerably from one company to another. However, each corporation, depending on its marketing strategy and current market position, values certain criteria differently. Therefore, sport marketers attempting to develop sponsorship proposals must understand the criteria and tailor proposals to specific sponsors.

Best Practices

FedEx's Sponsorship Recipe

With equal parts of local and national events with indirect revenue, FedEx has developed a portfolio framework that is integrated, actionable, and measurable and represents best practice in the field.

> The portfolio is segmented by objective, not price. Internal teams are divided into two complementary camps, not one. And sponsorships as a tactical discipline are used in no less than five very different ways. Other brands focus on businesses [b-to-b] or consumers [b-to-c], but FedEx has to keep both on the radar screen. Although the primary target is in the b-to-b world, the company must build its umbrella name inside the b-to-c universe to ensure one of the most ubiquitous brands maintains its leadership status. 'We are constantly reminding ourselves that we are not merely in the business of sponsoring things,' says managing director of sponsorships Kevin Demsky. 'We are in the business of convincing customers to utilize our services. Sponsorships are just a conduit to accomplishing the corporate objective.

> That conduit plays a pivotal role inside the marketing machine, as evidenced by the business FedEx signs at events, the revenue generated direct from properties, and the strategic way the company uses sponsorships to invade new markets and maintain presence in existing operating regions. Using sponsorships, [FedEx] penetrated new areas and grown share faster than we could have before. They create an anchor point in the marketing mix.

FedEx has eight rules for winning the game of sponsorships:

1. Sponsorships Are Not Created Equal

There are five corporate goals for sponsorships: Drive revenue; provide an opportunity to entertain customers in a unique environment; give sales a platform for developing relationships; create benefits for employees; and drive the brand.

FedEx marketers realize few sponsorships can score five-for-five. We recognize that not all properties can deliver on all goals.' Different sponsorships deliver on different objectives, and only when marketers acknowledge that can they develop a portfolio in which a series of properties achieve goals together. FedEx builds a collection of sponsorships that together helps move the needle.

2. Structure Portfolios by Objective, Not Price

If sponsorships are not created equal and can only achieve some of the five objectives, properties must be segmented into a portfolio that plays to the strengths and challenges of each. According to FedEx, 'Sponsorships deliver different benefits, so we've built a unique framework that allows us to see how our properties contribute.' It's a strategic framework for defining the different pieces of the portfolio in a way that allows the company to analyze and make decisions on performance. FedEx's uses a five-tier portfolio structure categorizes sponsorships by objective, instead of price.

Category 5: Hospitality Events. Sponsorships that create 'focused, private, extended' windows in which to invite customers to interact with FedEx. Such events are used to build relationships and learn more about prospects' businesses

Category 4: Hometown Events. Through acquisition, FedEx's home is no longer solely in Memphis. FedEx Ground is based in Pittsburgh. FedEx Custom Critical operates in Akron, OH. Category 4 sponsorships keep the brand visible in the communities where it affects economic and social areas.

Category 3: Key Targets. Put in place to affect a specific geographic region or a specific demographic target. 'For example, if our local marketing teams decide they need to penetrate Denver, my group will go out and set up a robust sponsorship plan to help drive business in that region.'

Category 2: Revenue & Supply Chain Events. FedEx partners with properties that integrate the company's services into its own operations. The integration is then used as a compelling case study to share with customers and prospects about how FedEx helps businesses run smoother. Direct revenue is a secondary benefit, as the property will buy FedEx services.

Category 1: Leadership Events. The crown jewels leveraged across multiple channels and used on a national basis to achieve most of the five corporate goals. 'We can do a little bit of everything with these events. This is the one category that, because we can do so many things, we invest in a variety of activation vehicles.'

In a system based on objectives, size doesn't matter. A FedEx Forum sits in Category 4, an NFL in Category 1, and a FedEx Field (used to invade the critical Washington, DC, market) in Category 3. 'The structure allows us to tailor our investments. Each property comes with a different set of expectations, and we calibrate our ROI calculation based on the category.'

3. Measure Independently

An organization that treats every sponsorship independently needs an ROI system that measures each property singularly.

The company is getting ready to come out of the closet with an Index Measurement Tool that will calculate specific ratings based on property performance. 'If we have a category model that recognizes no two sponsorships are the same, then we need a tool that will give us an accurate barometer to see if events are doing what we expect them to do.'

The tool involves an 'objective template' that is laid on top of sponsorships to generate a score that indicates if an event is performing. The different scores are then combined to gauge the performance of the overall portfolio. 'We don't expect a FedEx Field to have the same ROI as a PGA, so the Index Tool will help normalize the differences between properties and help us measure events on equal footing.'

If a property scores low, FedEx will meet with the partner and try to determine how to raise the number. If the score still remains low, it's an indication that the property may be ready for elimination from the portfolio.

4. Pass on Awareness

If a property primarily represents impressions, FedEx takes a pass—quickly. After all, with recognition near 100 percent, eyeballs are appreciated but not necessary.

'Certainly awareness is something that we are interested in creating, but only if it's a byproduct of a sponsorship. In the hierarchy of benefits that come from sponsorship investments, it's not high on our list of must-haves.'

More important are elements that push leads, anchor the brand, and provide face time. Impressions end up as icing on the sponsorship cake. 'This company is measured by how many packages are shipped, and our sponsorships are measured by their contribution in driving those shipments. It's too easy to get focused on how many eyeballs saw the brand that you lose focus on how many of those eyeballs pulled out their wallets.'

5. Sponsorships 'Plus-Up' the Mix

Smart marketers integrate sponsorships throughout the marketing mix, not the other way around. 'Certainly advertising, direct-response, and promotions are important on their own, but sponsorships provide a healthy way to plus-up the marketing mix beyond the events. Sponsorship is a tool in and of itself, but it's also a tool to make everything else a little bit better. We're now using sponsorships as a more strategic tool and recognizing that we can integrate our events throughout the entire mix.'

6. A House with Two Sides

Without a solid internal structure, sponsorships can't be identified, managed, and serviced. Keep it simple and focused by creating two sides to the sponsorship team: One manages the present, the other focuses on the future. Fed Ex has a core team of 11 in-house team members in its event department. One team is focused on activating and leveraging investments already made via marketing programs, promotional components, hospitality efforts, and so on. On the other side of the house is another team responsible for managing the growth of the portfolio. That team identifies new sponsorship opportunities, whether or not the portfolio has the right mix, and oversees all selection, planning, and negotiations. Each team has staffers attached to specific properties. They manage all aspects of the deals, working with rights-holders, as well as other FedEx business units that may leverage the sponsorships.

7. Make Hospitality a Marketing Extension

Hospitality elements provide a platform for live extensions of branding. A sport organization's tagline, images, thematics, and attributes should come alive on-site. FedEx ties hospitality to different umbrella marketing messages. The Super Bowl annually sports hospitality interactives tied to the Air & Ground offerings. PGA events are used to showcase FedEx's reliability. At Gillette Stadium, the company brought its new 'Relax. It's FedEx' tagline to life with a Relax Zone boasting soothing music, candles, and massages.

Hospitality must also be immersive. At the St. Jude Classic, for instance, FedEx erects a two-story structure that rivals any golf clubhouse. It's less about food and drinks, and more about isolated environments for building relationships. 'We've learned the average company employee doesn't have the authority to choose which company their employer uses to ship a package. And for those individuals that do have the authority, it's a complicated decision. So in order to help our salespeople get some time with those customers, we create the quality time in which to have a discussion.'

FedEx also makes the most of hospitality with off-hour events for customers and prospects. The company, for example, last winter created NFL Open Houses in five markets in which as many as 500 customers were brought in on an off day for activities, entertainment, behind-the-scenes tours, and chalk talks with players. The hospitality blueprint follows no less than Six Points of Communication with the target: pre-invite, formal 'save the date' invitation, a 'what to expect' message, itinerary, the on-site event, and a follow-up.

8. Say When

There's nothing wrong with window-shopping, but event marketers should know when the portfolio has had enough. 'If you have 20 properties that you need to actively leverage, you have too many properties.' If the return is not meeting objectives, then it may be more of an issue of which property is not delivering than which property needs to be added.

Cover Story: Game On. Event Marketer Retrieved June 22 from http://www.eventmarketermag.com/Article_Display.478+M54bde27910e.0.html Reprinted with permission

Additional Readings

Motion, J. Leitch, S., and Brodie, R. (2003). Equity in corporate co-branding. *European Journal of Marketing*, 37, (7/8), 1080-1094.

References

Amis, J., Pant, N., and Slack, T. (1997). Achieving a sustainable competitive advantage: A resource-based view of sport sponsorship. *Journal of Sport Management*, 11, 1, 80-95.

Amshay, T. & Brian, V. (1998, July 20-26). Sport sponsorship sword cuts both ways. *Sports Business Journal*, 23.

Baseball's Cubs run free funeral promotion (2004). Stadia. Retrieved from the World Wide Web May 21, 2004: http://www.stadia.tv.archive/user/news_article.tpl?id=20040521160041

Copeland, R., Frisby, W., and McCarville, R. (1996). Understanding the sport sponsorship from a corporate perspective. *Journal of Sport Management*, 10, 1, 32-48.

Cordiner, R. (2002, January). Sponsors of the wide world of sport—what's in it for them? *Sports Marketing*, 14-16.

Cordova, J. (1996). *Coca-Cola's Sponsorship Objectives*. Colorado Springs, CO: National Sports Forum.

Drehs, W. (2004). *Winston washed out in sea of yellow and black*. Retrieved February 12 from http://sports.espn.go.com/rpm/news/story?id=1733753.

Dunn, D. (2004). Personal interview June 18, Los Angeles, CA.

Ehrlich D. (1998, June 1-7). Sponsors target Cup's huge audience. *Sports Business Journal*, 26.

Evinrude renews long-term sponsorship of FLW Outdoors (2004). Retrieved July 2 from http//:www.sponsorship.com/news/content/5610.asp?source=iotw70104.

Five key factors that ensure relevant activation and sponsorship success (2004). *IEG Sponsorship Report*, 23 (11), 1-3.

Goldberg, R. (1998a, June 22-28). Co-branding ideal for sponsors who want to go the extra mile. *Sports Business Journal*, 22.

Goldberg, R. (1998b, June 22-28). Toughest task: Measuring results. *Sports Business Journal*, 29.

Graham, S. (1998, June 22-28). Rights deals making a play for sales value. *Sports Business Journal*, 34.

Green, E. (2002). *The Compaq Way*. Boston: 2002 National Sports Forum.

Greenwald, L., and Fernandez-Balboa, J. M. (1998). Trends in the sport marketing industry and in the demographics of the United States: Their effect on the strategic role of grassroots sport sponsorship in corporate America. *Sport Marketing Quarterly*, 7, 4, 35-48.

Hagstrom, R. G. (1998). *The NASCAR Way*. New York: Wiley.

Irwin, R. L., Assimakopoulos, M. K., and Sutton, W. A. (1994). A model for screening sport sponsorship opportunities. *Journal of Promotion Management*, 2, 3/4, 53-69.

Irwin, R. L., and Sutton, W. A. (1994). Sport sponsorship objectives: An analysis of their relative importance for major corporate sponsors. *European Journal of Sport Management*, 1, 2, 93-101.

Irwin, R., Lackowitz, T., Cornwell, B., and Clark, J. (2003). Cause-related sport sponsorship: An assessment of spectator beliefs, attitudes and behavioral intentions. *Sport Marketing Quarterly*, 12 (3), 131-137.

Johnson, G. (1998, April 21). Kids sports go commercial. *Akron Beacon Journal*, C7.

Joyce, M. (2003, June 23-29). Alt-sport execs see growth and growing pains for category's events and sponsors. *Sports Business Journal*, 8.

Keeping the Olympics' ideal (1997, April). *Sport Business*, 32-33.

King, B. (1998, August 17-23). Earnhardt wants to tune up your engine. *Sports Business Journal*, 9.

Kennet, P.A., Sneath, J. Z., and Erdmann, J. W. (1998, Winter). The quantitative and qualitative benefits of sponsoring the 1996 Olympics: An exploratory study. *International Sports Journal*, 115-126.

Kuzma, J. R., Shanklin, W. L., and McCally, J. F. (1993). Number one principle for sporting events seeking corporate sponsors: Meet benefactor's objectives. *Sport Marketing Quarterly*, 2 (3), 27-32.

Lauletta, S. (2003). Negotiations part one: Executives outline approach to say no to a prospective sponsor. *Team Marketing Report*, 15, (4), 8.

Lefton, T. (2003, October 27- November 2). Little league touches all the bases with four multi-year sponsorships. *Sports Business Journal*, 13.

Migala, D. (2004a). *Be a good host—How to increase revenue thought non-traditional hospitality outings*. Retrieved March 3 from http//:migialiareport.mar04-story2.cfm.

Migala, D. (2004b). *What's the buzz: Activation is the buzzword among marketers.* Retrieved March 3 from http//:migialiareport.mar04-story2.cfm.

McDonald, M. (1998). *Sport Sponsorship and the Role of Personality Matching.* Buffalo, NY: Conference of the North American Society for Sport Management.

Motion, J. Leitch, S., and Brodie, R. (2003). Equity in corporate co-branding. *European Journal of Marketing,* 37, (7/8), 1080-1094.

Muellner, A. (1998, August 3-9). Nike ups its investment in Miami community causes. *Sports Business Journal,* 8.

Nextel launches exclusive wireless service (2004). Retrieved June 28 from http://www.sponsorship.com/news/content/5593.asp?sources+iotw062804.

Pepsi wants bigger number of smaller multicultural properties (May 3, 2004). *IEG Sponsorship Report,* 23, (8), 1-3.

Performance Research (2004). *Sponsorship spending & decision making.* Retrieved March 3 from http://www.performanceresearch.com/sponsorship-spending.htm.

Pitts, B. G. (2003). *Banking on the pink dollar: Sponsorship and the gay games.* Sport Marketing Association Annual Conference, Gainesville, FL.

Ponturo, T. (2002). *What sponsors want.* Panel discussion, 2002 National Sports Forum, Pittsburgh, PA.

Product integration: Not just for technology companies anymore (May 3, 2004). Assertions. *IEG Sponsorship Report,* 23, (8), 1,3.

Reynolds, M. (1998, June 22-28). Women's sport: A growth area. *Sports Business Journal,* 30.

Ries, A., and Trout, J. (1986). *Positioning: The Battle for Your Mind.* New York: McGraw-Hill.

Rohm, A. (1997). The creation of consumers bonds within running. *Sports Marketing Quarterly,* 6, 2, 17-25.

Saunders, S. (1996). *Does It Sell Beer?* Colorado Springs, CO: National Sports Forum.

Seaver, R. (2004, January). *2004 Corporate Sponsorship Survey Report.* San Diego: Seaver Marketing Group.

Seaver, R. (1996, January) *Survey of the Industry.* San Diego: Seaver Marketing Group.

Sponsors reveal return on investment, (1997, March 31). *IEG Sponsorship Report,* 5.

Staying ahead of the Games: Visa banks and merchants post Olympic results (2004). *IEG Sponsorship Report,* 23, (14), 7.

Stotlar, D. K. (1999, January). Sponsorship in North America: A survey of sport executives. *Journal of Sport Marketing and Sponsorship,* 1, (1), 87-99.

Stotlar, D. K. (1997). *Xerox: A case study of Olympic sponsorship.* San Antonio, TX: Annual Conference of the North American Society for Sport Management.

Thwaites, D., and Aguilar-Manjarrez, R. (1997). *Sport Sponsorship Development Among Leading Canadian Companies.* Montpellier, France: Forth European Congress on Sport Management.

Ukman, L. (1997, January 17). *Assertions.* International Events Group. Retrieved January 23 from www.sponsorship.com.

Ukman, L. (2004a). *Return on Sponsorship.* Chicago: International Events Group.

Ukman, L. (May 3, 2004b). Assertions. *IEG Sponsorship Report,* 23, (8), 1-3

Ukman, L. (June 14 , 2004c). Assertions. *IEG Sponsorship Report,* 23, (11), 2.

University reaps high five figures from Homecoming sponsorship (2003). Retrieved November 17 from htpp://sponsorship.com/IEGR/2003/11/17/4710.asp.

Volvo and sport sponsorship. (1990, January 29). *Special Events Reports,* pp. 4-5.

Sponsor Needs Worksheets

The worksheets provide a guide for developing various sections of your sponsorship plan. The following sheets cover sponsor needs and rationale. Complete these worksheets as a preparatory step in the creation of a sponsorship plan.

Identify the demographics of your event or team and match them to those of your potential sponsor.

_____

_____

_____

_____

_____

_____

_____

_____

Determine the psychographic and image match between the sponsor's product and your property.

_____

_____

_____

_____

_____

Enumerate possible awareness objectives that could be accomplished through the sponsorship.

_____

_____

_____

_____

_____

Cite possible image objectives that could be accomplished through the sponsorship.

_____

_____

_____

_____

_____

Itemize possible sales objectives that could be accomplished through the sponsorship.

_____

_____

_____

_____

_____

Describe possible hospitality objectives that could be accomplished through the sponsorship.

_____

_____

_____

_____

_____

Present possible employee motivation objectives that could be accomplished through the sponsorship.

_____

_____

_____

_____

_____

_____

Determine and describe the potential for on-site sales and wholesaler tie-ins that could be accomplished through the sponsorship.

_____

_____

_____

_____

_____

Discuss the potential for cross-promotions possible through sponsorship.

_____

_____

_____

_____

Consider integrated communications potential issues regarding the timing of the sponsorship and the sponsor's business activities.

_____

_____

_____

_____

_____

List all current sponsors and reflect on any conflicts that may surface.

_____

_____

_____

_____

_____

Detail the nature of cooperation obtained from the venue/facility.

_____

_____

_____

_____

_____

Outline any conceivable risks that may result from the sponsorship.

_____

_____

_____

_____

_____

Discuss the potential of all cause-related sponsorship options.

_____

_____

_____

_____

_____

Determine whether any grassroots sponsorship options may be available for sponsors.

_____

_____

_____

_____

_____

Chapter Four

Olympic Sponsorship Opportunities

The Olympic Movement and Sponsorship

Olympic and amateur sport organizations have, over the past Olympiads, become increasingly dependent upon corporate sponsors who have supplied much-needed revenue in difficult financial times. The dependency of the Olympic movement on corporate sponsors is evidenced by the fact that about 30% of the International Olympic Committee's budget and 40% of the United States Olympic Committee's (USOC) funds are derived from sponsorship and licensing income. Specifically, for the period ending in 2002 the USOC had revenues totaling $129,521,000 with income from their joint sponsorship program of $29.6 million and royalty and rights fees at $10.2 million and $22.1 million respectively (United States Olympic Committee, 2002). Olympic Organizing Committees also increasingly depend on these resources. Sponsorship revenue for the 2002 Olympic Games accounted for 54% of all income. These sources accounted for 43% of the budget used to produce the Nagano Winter Olympic Games and were somewhat less of the budget for Sydney (34%) (Olympic Fact File, 1998; Olympic Fact File, 2000; International Olympic Committee, 2004b).

One aspect of the Olympic movement that has attracted sponsors is the global power represented in the Olympic symbol, the five interlocking rings. The Olympic Rings have been found to be the most recognizable logo in the world with 89.8% of the population capable of correctly recognizing the symbol (TOP IV Programme, 1997). Thus, associating with the Olympic Rings would be highly prized by leading corporations and could increase corporate exposure to the cumulative worldwide TV audience of 4 billion viewers who typically watch the Games either in-person or through the global television coverage (Olympic Fact File, 2004).

Sponsorship and the Olympic Games have existed since the Games' inception. In ancient Greece, city-states and merchants supported many athletes. With the revival of the Games in 1896, Kodak placed an ad in the official program of the first modern Olympics. It was in 1928 that Coca-Cola began its long-standing relationship with the Olympic movement (Pratzmark and Frey, 1989). Sponsorship and the Olympics have a well-established relationship and one that has significantly increased in complexity.

Commercialization of the Olympic Games

A transition was witnessed between the 1976 Montreal Olympic Games and the 1984 Los Angeles Games. Most people are aware of the intense financial burden (a debt of over $1 billion) that the 1976 Games placed on Montreal and the overt commercialization of the 1984 Games. Through their efforts in attracting corporate sponsors, the Los Angeles Olympic Organizing Committee was able to operate the Games and generate a profit in excess of $225 million.

> There [were] plenty of opportunities for sale in the five-ring circus: television, commercials, product licensing, product exclusivity at the Games, team sponsorships, Olympic movement sponsorships, awards presentations, training center support, product endorsements, and almost anything a marketing [person] could devise

(Marsano, 1987, p. 65). Since the commercialization in 1984 and the realization of substantial profits, sponsorship has become an integral part of the Olympic movement.

Corporate rationale for Olympic sponsorship is quite similar to the rationale for other sponsorship activities. Carter and Wilkinson (2002) explored sponsor rationale for the 2000 Sydney Games. They found that the top-ranked objective was increasing brand awareness followed by reaching an appropriate audience, showcasing products, and increasing employee morale. Results from their study showed that hospitality objectives were ranked somewhat lower than in other studies. It is important to note that there was significant variance on these factors and the level of sponsorship demonstrating that different sponsors sought different objectives. Furthermore, the literature (cited earlier) indicates that high levels variance also exists between sponsoring companies.

Olympic Sponsorship Rights and Privileges

There are five different types of Olympic sponsorships in which corporations could become involved: National Governing Bodies, National Olympic Committees, Olympic Organizing Committees, the IOC's worldwide Olympic sponsorship program, and the International Olympic Committee itself. Each entity provides specific sponsor rights associated with participation.

National Governing Bodies

At the base of the Olympic organization the National Governing Bodies (NGBs) have engaged in a variety sponsorship activities. Each Olympic sport has an NGB in each country that is a member of the IOC. These organizations can grant sponsorship rights to companies for activities for their sport within a single country. For sponsors of NGBs, it is important to understand that they can gain access to the team members of that sport, the uniforms of that sport, and the NGB's logo, but not the Olympic Rings. US Skiing has successfully managed their sponsorship programs for many years, independently from the USOC. In preparation for the 2002 Olympic Games in Salt Lake City, US Skiing commented "we try to work with their sponsors when we can, but we have signed nothing over" (Ukman, 1997, p. 2).

USA Gymnastics continues to work with Olympic sponsor VISA. The two signed an agreement for 2005-2008 for VISA to be the title sponsor of the USA Gymnastics Championships (to be called the VISA Championships). Through the sponsorship VISA also becomes the official payment sponsor. USA Gymnastics President Bob Colarossi said "VISA has been a valuable contributor and marketing partner for the organization and we look forward to another successful Olympic quadrennium together as we jointly develop programs for the 2008 Beijing Olympic Games" (Eaton, 2004).

The US Soccer Federation recently signed Nike to a 10-year sponsorship worth $120 million. Their agreement stipulates that Nike will support youth development programs and provide equipment and uniforms to all US national teams. Nike also secured deals with soccer governing bodies in several other nations, including some of the world's top teams (Netherlands, Brazil, Nigeria, and South Korea). Miller Brewing Company also teamed up with a national governing body when it signed up as a sponsor for the Mexican National Soccer Team to promote its brands in Mexico.

Several successful NGB sponsorship arrangements were consummated for the Athens Olympic Games. Nautica International signed up as the official apparel supplier for US Sailing. Through the arrangement Nautica supplied outfits for the 130 members of the US Sailing Team, the US Disabled Sailing Team, and the US Sailing World Youth Team ("Nautica signs," 2004).

Another NGB, USA Team Handball, created a rather unique sponsorship opportunity. Team Handball created an innovative program where individual citizens and schools could "adopt" a USA Team Handball team member for the Olympic Games. "Adoption papers" cost only $35.00 per athlete and brought much-needed funding to USA Team Handball. In addition, it generated a significant amount of publicity and created excitement about the sport in numerous communities across the country.

National Olympic Committees

A National Olympic Committee (NOC) can authorize the use of the Olympic rings, but only in conjunction with their respective logo. For the United States Olympic Committee (USOC), that would mean using the designated symbols of the USOC as defined in their graphic standards manual. The most frequently used USOC symbol depicts the Olympic Rings accompanied by the letters USA. Any USOC logo must, of course, adhere to the rigorous specifications outlined by the USOC. For the quadrennium ending in 2004, the USOC secured sponsorships at the "Partner" level, the highest with the USOC, from AT&T, Anheuser-Busch, General Motors, Bank of America, and ChevronTexaco. All domestic partners, sponsors, and suppliers receive marketing rights to the U.S. Olympic Team and commercial access to Olympic themes, terminology and imagery for use in sponsor marketing and advertising programs. These sponsors would have the right to proclaim themselves as USOC sponsors and sponsors of the US Olympic Team. According to the USOC "the 'Sponsor' level represents the level of corporate support required to gain access to the USA-5 ring logo as an 'Official Sponsor' and commercial access to Olympic themes, terminology and imagery for use in sponsor marketing programs." USOC Sponsors provide significant levels of cash, products, or services in support of the U.S. Olympic Team and may also choose to extend their U.S. Olympic investment to include National NGBs, the U.S. Paralympic Team, and/or U.S. Olympic Signature Property events and programs. Sponsors at this level include such companies as All State Insurance, Kellogg, Home Depot, Hallmark, Office Depot, PowerBar, United Airlines, and 24 Hour Fitness, among others. PowerBar supplied more than 600,000 energy bars to the U.S. Olympic Team over the past few years, as the "Official Nutritional Energy Bar Supplier" for the U.S. Olympic Team. An array of other companies has bought in at the "Supplier" level that provides access only to the USOC Supplier logo that also includes the rings. "All domestic partners, sponsors, and suppliers receive marketing rights to the U.S. Olympic Team and conduct all advertising and marketing programs within the U.S." (United States Olympic Committee, 2004).

Motivations driving the USOC sponsorship vary. Bank of America's chief marketing officer commented,

The Olympic Games are watched by a broad and diverse audience of Americans, and we expect the 2008 Olympic Games in Beijing will draw record television ratings in the United States and worldwide. As the nation's largest consumer bank, and one with corporate clients in more than 150 countries, the Olympic Games enable our brand to reach hundreds of millions of consumers and corporate customers

(Bank of America, 2004). Value-in-kind was a great benefit of the USOC's arrangement with ChevronTexaco during the 2004 Athens Olympic Games. The USOC had budgeted over $1 million for accommodations for its officials, yet was able to secure a cruise ship from Royal Olympic by providing fuel received as part of their sponsorship with ChevronTexaco (Woodward, 2004).

Because the 2002 Olympic Games were held in the United States (Salt Lake City), the USOC developed a new marketing and sponsorship program in 1998 entitled Olympic Properties of the United States (OPUS). This program was designed with constructs similar to those of the ACOP program administered for the 1996 Atlanta Games. This program provided access to the benefits offered by the USOC together with properties associated with the Salt Lake Organizing Committee. One of the new sponsors signed up by OPUS was General Motors. The $1 billion eight-year deal allowed GM to market a variety of vehicles to the diverse audience that the Olympic Games represented and to introduce new models in conjunction with the launch of each Olympic Games during the contract period (Rozin, 1998).

Interestingly, the Olympic Training Centers around the US are responsible for securing their own sponsorship arrangements. However, in most cases, they work very closely with the USOC marketing and sponsorship division. Many of the Olympic Training Center agreements encompass in-kind donations of products and services.

Olympic Organizing Committees

The Olympic Organizing Committees (OOCs) have also benefited from both television revenues and from sponsorship agreements. Beginning in 2004, Olympic TV rights revenues were shared on the basis of 49% to the OOC and 51% to the Olympic movement. The specific breakout specifies that the IOC share revenues with the international federations (IFs) for the Summer and Winter sports. In 2002, the Winter IFs received $85.8 million and in 2004 the Summer Games IFs got $224 million. A review of the TV rights fees paid by US broadcasting companies has been provided at the conclusion of this chapter. As noted earlier, as much as 50% of an organizing committee's budget may be generated through sponsorships. The rights involved with an organizing committee may include official suppliers, sponsors, and licensing agreements. The 2000 Sydney Games brought in $492 million from its partnerships while Salt Lake City brought in $876 million (International Olympic Committee, 2004).

The organizing committee is able to reduce budget demands through the value-in-kind (VIK) supplies and the sponsor is able to associate its products/services with the Games. Some of the more traditional examples include the sponsorship of awards, transportation, communication systems, and various sport-specific equipment. Ventures such as these have been very popular with both organizing committees and sponsors.

The Olympic Partners

In 1985, the IOC originated a program to make the world's most complicated sport marketing purchase a "one-stop shopping" venture for international corporations (Marsano, 1987, p. 65). No longer would companies endure the trauma of multiple negotiations that often produced only narrow results. What ensued was The Olympic Programme (TOP—now entitled The Olympic Partners). The first TOP program covered 1985-1988, TOP II provided sponsors with benefits from 1989-1992 and TOP III regulated sponsor activity from 1990-1996. Similarly, TOP IV's time frame included the 1998 Nagano Olympic and the 2000 Olympic Games in Sydney. TOP V covered the Winter Games of 2002 in Salt Lake City and the 2004 Summer Games in Athens and brought in an estimated $602 million (Olympic Fact File, 2004).

The system was patterned after the success of the Los Angeles Games, which demonstrated that having fewer sponsors, who paid more money, was better for organizers and sponsors alike. TOP established a system whereby a limited number of sponsors would receive special treatment and benefits on a worldwide basis while achieving product category exclusivity and protection for their Olympic sponsorship activities. Specifically, TOP Sponsors receive the following benefits (International Olympic Committee, 2004):

1. Product Exclusivity—Only one sponsor is allowed for any product category. This means that as long as Coca-Cola and VISA are members of the TOP, then Pepsi and American Express will not be allowed to become involved with Olympic sponsorship on any level, international, national, or with the Organizing Committee.

2. Use of Olympic Marks, Imagery, and Designations—Each participant is granted the right to use the solitary Olympic rings as well as use of the rings in combination with all 202 NOC designations. This provides both worldwide and local impact. Companies can also use the "Official Sponsor" and "Official Product" designations for all Organizing Committees in addition to the OOC logos.

3. Public Relations and Promotional Opportunities—Sponsors are given special tie-ins and media events to increase their exposure.

4. Access to Olympic Archives—The IOC makes available to sponsors articles, photographs, and video footage from the Olympic museum and archives in Switzerland for special exhibits and displays.

5. Olympic Merchandise and Premiums—Clothing and apparel can be used bearing the Olympic logos for sales incentives and marketing activities organized by each sponsor.

6. Tickets and Hospitality—Sponsors receive priority access to seating at both the Winter and Summer Games.

7. Advertising Options—Each participant in TOP is given first chance at souvenir program ads and the "right of first refusal" in purchasing advertising on Olympic broadcasts.

8. On-Site Participation—Point-of-purchase and product display are included in the package. Companies gain certain rights to concession areas

and space for product sampling. Showcase opportunities are also made available on the Olympic venue grounds.

9. Research—Each sponsor receives a full research report on the public's reception of their participation and an assessment of the value-added benefits.

10. First Right of Negotiation for the Next Quadrennial—All worldwide sponsors with TOP have the option to continue in their product category.

The nine initial clients in the TOP I program contributed a total of $95 million in revenues. For sponsors, TOP I proved to be a resounding success in 1988. Subsequently, the program produced $175 million for TOP II, $350 for TOP III and $500 million for TOP IV ending with the Sydney Games (TOP IV Programme, 1997). The TOP V program covering the 2002 Winter Games in Salt Lake City and the 2004 Summer Games in Athens generated over $650 million, with TOP VI slated to cover Torino in 2006 and Beijing in 2008.

TOP V companies and their representative categories, through the Athens Olympic Games, included (International Olympic Committee, 2004):

Company	Category
Coca-Cola	Nonalcoholic Beverage
Athos Origin	Information Technology
John Hancock	Life Insurance/Annuities
Kodak	Film/Photography & Imaging
VISA	Consumer Payment Systems
Panasonic-Matsushita	TV/Video/Audio Equipment
Samsung	Wireless Communications Equipment
McDonald's	Retail Food Services
Swatch	Timing, Scoring, and Venue Results Services
Lenovo	Computing Technology

Kodak was actually an advertiser in the program for the first Olympics of the modern era in 1896 and Coca-Cola became a supplier for the Olympics in 1928. Many of the others joined in 1988 when the TOP program was initiated while Samsung and McDonald's signed-up as members of the TOP IV program in 1997. The arrangement with Samsung provides the 1998 and 2000 Games with wireless communications equipment. This asset was deemed to be "vital to the achievement of a smooth and successful running of the Games" ("Two New Partners," 1997, 9). In addition, they provided over 20,000 cellular telephones to officials and participating teams. Another unique service was their "call home" program to allowed athletes to contact their families immediately after their events ("Worldwide TOP Programme," 1998). Samsung's Group President remarked, "The Olympic spirit of world peace and contribution to society is at one with Samsung's ideals ("Olympic Fact File," 1998, p. 54).

McDonald's decided to expand its 1996 sponsorship activities, which were limited to 10 countries, yet had an immense presence in Atlanta's Olympic Village. The International Olympic Committee was interested in securing McDonald's because they represent the largest foodservice retailer in the world serving 47 million people per day from 30,000 restaurants in over 100 countries. For McDonald's, the rationale was customer oriented, "Now all of our customers around the world can share in the fun and excitement of the Olympic Games ("Olympic Fact File," 1998, p. 53). McDonald's leveraged its Worldwide Partner status with the Canadian Olympic Committee by supporting Olympic School Day runs across Canada prior to the Games. Other global activities included a European program called "Go Active" featuring the promotion of adult happy meals with salad, water, and free stepometer. In China they featured cups with Olympic athletes and in Japan, they ran an Olympic-themed game with instant win coupons and premium prizes. Swatch joined in 2003 and Lenovo joined in 2004 for the 2006-2008 quadrennium.

The disbursement policy provides that revenues derived from the TOP program be shared. The proportion of revenues allocated to the various Olympic entities is as follows (Greater TOP support, 1999; Michel, 1991; International Olympic Committee, 2004):

- 40% of the funds are allotted to the participating National Olympic Committees. The precise distribution is based on a formula whereby the money is divided with each NOC receiving a set dollar amount (minimum of $40,000) plus an additional amount per athlete qualifying for the games.
- 50% of the funds are disbursed to the participating Olympic Organizing Committees. Within these parameters, the Winter Games Organizing Committee receives 10% of the monies while the Summer Games Organizing Committee is allotted 40%.
- The IOC keeps the remaining 10% ("Marketing issues," 1997; International Olympic Committee, 2004).

The corporations involved in TOP have a significant involvement in the Games and present a myriad of justifications and explanations for their participation (12 top companies, 1991; Worldwide TOP Programme, 1998; "Olympic Fact File," 1998; International Olympic Committee, 2002b).

John Hancock—As a company that offers a wide range of insurance and financial services, John Hancock plans to focus on athletes and grassroots promotions. In addition, during the 1998 Nagano Winter Olympics, they highlighted a cause-related campaign to rebuild sport facilities in war-torn Sarajevo. John Hancock's President noted, "The support of the athletes, clubs and clinics gives hometown America a chance to share the Olympic spirit" ("Olympic Fact File," 1998, p. 52)

Coca-Cola—The Olympic Games present a variety of opportunities for Coke. They continue to sponsor the Olympic Torch Relay and the popular on-site Olympic Pin Trading Centre. To promote their products, Coke supplies the Olympic village with "no charge" vending machines and has exclusive pouring rights for beverages at Olympic venues. Coke's Board of Directors Chair said, "As a global company, we feel it is important for us to be a part of such a powerful movement" ("Olympic Fact File," 1998, p. 51).

Kodak—Kodak has been part of the Olympic movement from the beginning of the modern Games. Kodak products were advertised in the book of official results for the first Olympiad of the modern era—Athens, 1896. Kodak's Olympic tradition continues with multiple goals. Those goals are, in simplest terms, building a positive image for Kodak, its products and its employees; promoting the highest ideals of sportsmanship; and fostering friendly competition among nations.

"Kodak is in the business of capturing and sharing moments and few events create positive memories quite like the Olympic Games ("Kodak and the Games," 2004). In support of these goals, Kodak operated the world's largest photo lab at the 2004 Athens Games providing digital and film processing for professional photographers and spectators alike. Accredited photographers used the 18,000 sq. ft. main media center and Kodak Picturemaker kiosks were located around the venues to assist spectators with their photographic needs allowing them to "instantly share their digital photos with friends and family around the world" ("Kodak and the Games," 2004). In addition, Kodak teamed with another sponsor Athos Origin to produce the 350,000 accreditation badges needed for the Games.

VISA—This sponsorship has been of immense benefit to the VISA brand and overall image. As noted elsewhere in this workbook (Chapter 9), VISA has gained substantial market share through their Olympic involvement. They have been very successful through advertising that highlights their exclusive vendor position with Olympic ticket sales. As a part of their TOP program, they established special VISA NET systems to link thousands of ATMs in over 200 countries. They have also supported a variety of the cultural and educational exhibits during the Games. The benefit of Olympic sponsorship for VISA was activating a

> powerful tool to help us achieve our objectives of building the VISA brand and providing our members and merchants with opportunities to build their business. . . No single sponsorship property has delivered stronger returns for our members and merchants than the Olympic Games

(VISA USA, 2004).

Panasonic—The Olympic Games provide an opportunity for Panasonic to showcase its technology as the principal contractor for the International Broadcast Centre (IBC). The IBC is the facility from which all television signals emanate. In addition to the IBC, Panasonic provides more than 20 giant screens and video-on-demand units at various locations in the Olympic host city. The rationale provided by Panasonic's President centered on having their corporate name "associated with this premier international athletic event" ("Olympic Fact File," 1998, p. 53).

TOP has served two major goals of the Olympic movement. It has made the IOC less dependent on television revenues and it has assisted all countries in the world with sport development through a shared revenue system.

Paralympics

Another Olympic-related event is the Paralympic Games. These events (Summer and Winter) follow the regularly scheduled Olympic Games by two weeks and provide competition for the world's elite disabled athletes. This differs appreciably from the Special Olympics, which provides opportunities for mentally disabled participants. The Paralympics have been extremely successful in showcasing the talents of elite athletes with disabilities such as blindness, amputation, or paralysis.

> The first Paralympics were held in 1960 in Rome, Italy. Only 400 athletes from 23 countries participated. It wasn't until the 1988 Paralympics in Seoul, Korea, that the modern-day practice of the Olympic-host nation

also hosted the Paralympic Games. Today more than 4,000 athletes from 120 countries participate in the Summer Paralympics, while more than 1,100 athletes from 36 countries compete in the Winter Paralympic Games (http://www.usparalympics.org/usparalympics.htm). The US Paralympic team's mission is "to be the world leader in the Paralympic movement by developing comprehensive and sustainable elite programs integrated into Olympic National Governing Bodies. To utilize our Olympic and Paralympic platform to promote excellence in the lives of persons with disabilities" (http://www.usparalympics.org/usparalympics.htm).

As an affiliate of the USOC, ties with USOC sponsors are strong; however, the US Paralympic organization has the right to pursue sponsorship independently. In 2004, just prior to the Athens Olympics, the US Paralympic team secured a sponsorship from DaimlerChrysler Vans as their official vehicle sponsor. DaimlerChrysler is working with Olympic gold medalist Chris Waddell to reach out to rehabilitation hospitals across the US through a multiple city tour. Although General Motors in an official sponsor of the USOC, they did not have the funds to support the US Paralympic team for Athens. In conversations with GM, US Paralympic Executive Director Charlie Hubner was granted permission to seek support from DaimlerChrysler for 2004. GM agreed to support the Paralympic team through the 2008 Beijing Games. Similarly, TOP sponsor John Hancock allowed US Paralympics to pursue and secure The Hartford as their insurance sponsor, based in part on The Hartford's long time association with disabled sport.

Both Bank of America and Nike who sponsor the USOC also contribute to the US Paralympic team. The division of funds between the USOC and Paralympics in handled internally, but the support is significant to the US Paralympic team's success. The USOC provides other funding for the US Paralympic team, but the funding provided for Paralympic athletes is substantially less than that provided for the able-bodied Olympic athletes and increases the need to the organization to seek sponsors independently.

Ambush Marketing

As the cost of obtaining sponsorship rights with sport organizations began to escalate, some companies started to explore methods that could deliver the same impact as a sport sponsorship, but at a reduced cost. Some corporate marketers decided they would attempt to associate their company with sport events without paying the requisite sponsorship fee. This tactic soon became known as *Ambush Marketing*. Ambush marketing has been defined as "a promotional strategy whereby a non-sponsor attempts to capitalize on the popularity/prestige of a property by giving the false impression that it is a sponsor. [This tactic is] often employed by the competitors of a property's official sponsors" (Ukman, 1995, p. 42). Several prominent examples of ambush marketing have developed within the sport industry.

At the 1984 Olympic Games, Kodak cleverly ambushed Fuji Film. Although Fuji had purchased the right to be an official sponsor from the Los Angeles Olympic Organizing Committee, but the public was convinced that Kodak, not Fuji, was the official sponsor (Marsano, 1987). By purchasing sponsorships with the

USOC and buying numerous television ads during the Games, Kodak created the perception that they were an official sponsor of the Olympic Games. Kodak did not mislead the public, but merely leveraged the public's ignorance about the recently conceived Olympic sponsorship concept.

In some instances, the Olympic organizers are partially to blame for allowing ambush marketing activities. In an effort to commemorate the Games, the Los Angeles City Council approved a name-change for one of their thoroughfares to "Olympic Boulevard." As a result, hundreds of business relocated to the street and opened up businesses with names like Olympic Cleaners, Olympic Limousines, etc. These measures were deemed to be legal because businesses were allowed, under city statute, to use their street location name as part of their business identity.

Nike cleverly had murals painted on the sides of assorted downtown Los Angeles buildings during the Games (Myerson, 1996). The same strategy was averted in Atlanta when the City Council passed a ban on large-scale outdoor advertising. Reebok officials unsuccessfully argued that their proposed 60-by-80 foot mural of Shaquille O'Neal was public art. However, several companies discovered a loophole since the regulations did not include large portable signage or building-sized projected images (Bayor, 1996).

American Express and VISA have had continuous battles over legitimate sponsorship rights and alleged ambush tactics since 1988. VISA aired advertising that claimed that the Olympics would not take American Express cards. This was technically accurate in reference to the official ticket outlets. However, various tour companies and other travel-related services would accept American Express cards in payment. During the 1992 Barcelona Games, American Express constructed it own advertising campaign that claimed that you did not need a Visa (as opposed to VISA card) to go to Barcelona. Note that no mention was made of the Olympic Games. As a final ploy in their strategy, American Express purchased sponsorship rights to the hotel key fobs at the IOC headquarters hotel. The key fobs were shaped and colored like an American Express card on one side with hotel information on the other.

Ambush marketing tactics are not confined to overzealous corporations. The City of Atlanta Convention and Visitors Bureau tried to sell sponsorships during the 1996 Games in conflict with the ACOP program. They were, however, bought-off by ACOP for $3 million. Former IOC Vice President Dick Pound commented "It never occurred to anybody that a city would ever think of ambushing its own organizing committee' (Wells, 1996, p. 53). The IOC was so concerned that some citizens believed ambush marketing was clever or inspired that they began using the term *parasite marketing* to convey a less-than-positive impression of the practice. Protection against this type of ambush is now required in the bid documents submitted for consideration in hosting the Games. Beijing enacted the Olympic Signs Protection Act that came into effect on April 1, 2002. Any infringement of the rules would first be dealt with through an order for cessation followed by confiscation and destruction of goods. Furthermore, the offender is required to forfeit all profits and could be fined up to five times the estimated profits (Chua, 2002).

There is some concern that the IOC is not "practicing what it preaches." In 1994 the IOC developed its own program for IOC sponsors (as opposed to Worldwide Olympic sponsors). The IOC sold an automobile sponsorship to Mercedes-Benz and an airline deal to Lufthansa, among others. According to one industry leader "We always thought it a bit underhanded that the International Olympic Committee had its own sponsors" (Ukman, 1998, p. 2).

The IOC, USOC, NGBs, sponsors, and networks have worked diligently to curtail ambush marketing of the Games. In 1996, the Atlanta Organizing Committee, together with the IOC, established a fund to publicize the names of ambush marketers in national newspapers. The advertising copy stated that "Deceptive advertising is not an Olympic sport," and "Every time a company runs an ad like this, our Olympic team loses" (Myerson, 1996, p. D1). These funds were not used and the threat seems to have had the desired results. Currently, the IOC requires the bid cities to enact legislation of control the illegal use of IOC and OOC marks. The IOC reported that since 1996 the Olympics have been relatively free from ambush marketing activities.

References

12 top companies. (1991, February). *The Magazine of the Organizing Committee of the XVI Winter Games*, pp. 44-45.

Ambush marketing: Under control in Nagano. (1998, Summer). *Olympic Marketing Matters*, 9.

Bank of America announces US Olympic Team sponsorship through 2008 Olympic Games. (2004). Retrieved from the World Wide web on May 17 from http://www.sponsorship.com/News/Content/5411.asp?source=iotw051704.

Bayor, L. (1996, May 20). Atlanta fends off megasigns. *Advertising Age*, 30.

Carter, L., and Wilkinson, I. (2002). *Reasons for sponsoring the Sydney 2000 Olympic Games*. ANZMAC 2000 Visionary Marketing for the 21st Century: Facing the Challenge.

Chua, Y. (2002, Jul/Aug). China moves to protect Olympic insignia. *Managing Intellectual Property*, 121, p. 56.

Eaton, B. (2004, May 19). *VISA USA strengthens ties with USA Gymnastics through 2008*. Retrieved from the World Wide web on May 21 from http://www.sponsorship.com/News/Content/5424.asp?source=iotw052004.

Greater TOP support (1999, January). *Olympic Marketing Matters*, 10.

International Olympic Committee (2004). *2004 Marketing Fact File*. Lausanne: International Olympic Committee.

Kodak and the Games: A legacy of support (2004). Retrieved July 19 from http://sponsorship.com/news/content/5675.asp?source=iotw071904.

Marketing issues (1997, Summer). *Olympic Marketing Matters*, 2-3.

Marsano, W. (1987, September). *A Five Ring Circus*. Northwest, p. 64-69.

Michel, A. (1991). *Economics of the 1992 Albertville Olympics*. International Sport Business Conference, Columbia, S.C. February 28 - March 1.

Myerson, A. R. (1996, May 31) *Olympic sponsors battling to defend turf.* New York Times, D1, D17.

Nautica signs apparel Sponsorship with US Sailing teams (2004, May 21). Retrieved May 21 from http://www.sponsorship.com/News/Content/5425.asp?source=iotw052004

Olympic Fact File (1998). Lausanne: International Olympic Committee.

Olympic Fact File (2000). Lausanne: International Olympic Committee.

Olympic Fact File (2004). Lausanne: International Olympic Committee.

Pollack, J. (1996, May 20). Kraft teams up brands for Olympic sponsorship. *Advertising Age*, 30.

Pratzmark, R. R., and Frey, N. (1989, January). The Winners Play a New Global Game. *Marketing Communications*, pp. 18-27.

Rozin, S. (1998, February 21). Why corporate support is good business. *Forbes Special Advertising Section*.

Salt Lake Organizing Committee (1998, September 18). *Salt Lake 2002: Basic Plan for the XIX Olympic Games*. Salt Lake City: Salt Lake Organizing Committee.

TOP IV Programme (1997, Summer). *Olympic Marketing Matters*, 8.

Two new Partners (1997, Summer). *Olympic Marketing Matters*, 9.

Ukman, L. (1995). *IEG's Complete Guide to Sponsorship*. Chicago: International Events Group.

Ukman, L. (1997, August 18). Assertions. *IEG Sponsorship Report*, 2.

Ukman, L. (1998, October 26). Assertions. *IEG Sponsorship Report*, 2.

United States Olympic Committee (2002) *2002 Annual Report*. Colorado Springs: United States Olympic Committee.

United States Olympic Committee (2004). Retrieved July 2 from http://www.usolympicteam.com/12958.htm.

VISA USA making the most of 2004 Olympic Games with marketing campaign. (2004, March 31, Visa press release.) San Francisco: VISA USA, press release.

Wells, J. (1996, June 10). The big money man. *Macleans*, 52-56

Woodward, S. (2004, March 22-28. Allsate unveils HOF sponsorship. *Sports Business Journal*, 11.

World Wide Partners, (1999, January). *Olympic Marketing Matters*, 7.

Worldwide TOP programme, (1998, January). *Olympic Marketing Matters*, 8.

U.S. Television Rights Fees for the Olympic Games

Year	Site	Network	Price
1960	Squaw Valley (Winter)	CBS	$394,000
1960	Rome (Summer)	CBS	$550,000
1964	Innsbruck (Winter)	ABC	$597,000
1964	Tokyo (Summer)	NBC	$1.5 million
1968	Grenoble (Winter)	ABC	$2.5 million
1968	Mexico City (Summer)	ABC	$4.5 million
1972	Sapporo (Winter)	NBC	$6.4 million
1972	Munich (Summer)	ABC	$7.5 million
1976	Innsbruck (Winter)	ABC	$10 million
1976	Montreal (Summer)	ABC	$25 million
1980	Lake Placid (Winter)	ABC	$15.5 million
1980	Moscow (Summer)	NBC	$87 million
1984	Sarajevo (Winter)	ABC	$91.5 million
1984	Los Angeles (Summer)	ABC	$225 million
1988	Calgary (Winter)	ABC	$309 million
1988	Seoul (Summer)	NBC	$300 million
1992	Albertville (Winter)	CBS	$243 million
1992	Barcelona (Summer)	NBC	$401 million
1994	Lillehammer (Winter)	CBS	$300 million
1996	Atlanta (Summer)	NBC	$456 million
1998	Nagano (Winter)	CBS	$375 million
2000	Sydney (Summer)	NBC	$705 Million
2002	Salt Lake City (Winter)	NBC	$545 Million
2004	Athens (Summer)	NBC	$793 Million
2006	Turin (Winter)	NBC	$613 Million
2008	Beijing	NBC	$894 Million
2010	Vancouver (Winter)	NBC	$820 Million
2012	TBD	NBC	$1.18 Billion

Chapter Five

Individual Athlete Sponsorships

Introduction

In ancient times, like the 1960s, few athletes were able to obtain individual sponsorship deals. There were salaries for professional players and prize money for tournament winners, yet endorsements were few and far between. Big name players in golf like Arnold Palmer, Gary Player and Jack Nicklaus or tennis stars such as Billie Jean King and Stan Smith accorded attention and secured sponsorship deals. However, in 1972, a young attractive swimmer (who shall remain nameless) won seven gold medals in the Olympics and proceeded to price himself out of the business. This marked a turbulent time in the individual endorsement arena. However, the 1980s marked a revolution in athlete endorsements. The shoe and equipment companies literally fought over the top players and endorsement fees escalated through the mid '90s. However, when a recession hit the shoe industry in the later part of the decade, many of the companies reduced the number of athletes receiving large endorsement fees. The result was that while fewer players actually received contracts, the size of the contract for each athlete increased. The market rebounded in the early 2000s and in 2004 Nike committed $1.63 billion (current and future contracts) to player endorsements while rival Reebok encumbered $200 million in long-term commitments.

Brooks and Harris (1998) provided a conceptual framework through which sport marketers could examine athletic endorsements. They set forward four classifications of endorsement protocol. The first category was "(a) the explicit mode (I endorse this product), (b) the implicit mode (I use this product), (c) the imperative mode (You should use this product), and (d) the co-present mode (the athlete merely appears in some setting with the product)" (Brooks & Harris, 1998, p. 36). Stone, Joseph, and Jones (2003) forwarded several factors that corporations should evaluate before selecting athletes for endorsements. They suggest that the athlete should be high in trustworthiness, be easily recognizable by the target audience, be affordable for the sponsor, present little risk of negative publicity and be well matched with the product. Substantial research has also been done that shows how the fit between and athlete and the products that s/he endorse is critical factor. Below, several examples illustrate these points.

Endorsements

The lure of sport personalities has been present for decades. Just as Arnold Palmer and Jack Nicklaus speak to one generation, Tony Hawk and Dave Mira speak to another; endorsement money continues to exist. Both Nicklaus and Palmer (Arnold that is) continue to appear in commercial messages. However, those commercials are more than likely targeted to aging baby-boomers who have faith in the recommendation of their once favorite sports stars. Skateboarder Tony Hawk has secured endorsement contracts estimated at $10 million per year and his video game is the top selling sports game and number three of all video games sold. Dave Mira has his own BMX video game contract and a $700,000 endorsement with adidas (Bennett, Henson, & Zhang, 2002; Goldman, 2000).

Michael Jordan defined sport endorsements when he was with the National Basketball Association's (NBA) Chicago Bulls. He serves as the classic example of the way in which a player can build capital through salaries and sponsorship agreements. With a $28 million contract for his playing ability, Jordan could have probably survived. But when his contracts from outside endorsements and sponsorships were included, he might even have been considered wealthy. Jordan signed an endorsement deal with Nike worth $20 million per year and when combined with his other (MCI, Gatorade, Hanes, Rayovac, to name a few) endorsements, his non-salary earnings rose to $45 million per year in his last year of play (Spiegel, 1998).

Tiger Woods signed a contract with Nike immediately following his final amateur match. The five-year, $40 million Nike contract was one of the most lucrative in sport endorsement history. In addition, Titleist secured Woods as a spokesperson for five years at an estimated $20 million. His other early arrangements included $2 million from Rolex and $3 million per year from American Express. After winning the 1997 Master's, he also signed an agreement with Electronic Arts for a video game bearing his name. Tiger Woods renegotiated his contracts after the 2000 season (PGA Championship, US Open, British Open, Canadian Open) wins for a $100-million, 5-year contract with Nike plus others totaling $40 million (5 yr 2004-2009) from Buick, and he replaced Rolex with Tag Heuer; about 11 companies in all totaling $78 million per year in earnings (Isidore, 2004a).

Is he worth it? The financial data would seem to support the investment. 2004 Nike golf sales were estimated at $500 million, up 500% from 1997. Nike golf representative Dean Stoyer said, "Nobody can move product like Tiger can" (Isidore, 2004a).

Tiger Woods is clearly the leader in athlete endorsements. Eighty-eight percent of Americans know who Tiger is and 39% rank him as their favorite athlete (Isidore, 2004a). However, the influence of celebrity endorsers has been debatable. One survey showed only 4% of consumers said it was very important that a famous person endorsed a product (Schlossberg, 1990). Other data indicated that over 50% of the public thought athletes did it just for the money (Veltri, 1996). Furthermore, Veltri's (1996) research indicated that with the exception of Michael Jordan (and assuredly now, Tiger), few people were able to match an athlete endorser and the products that s/he endorsed. In general, basketball players were more often accurately recognized and male endorsers were more likely to be recognized than were female athletes (Veltri, 1996).

In the shadow of NBA legend Michael Jordan, rising star LeBron James earned over US$100 million in endorsements during his 2004 rookie season, most notably from his seven-year US$90 million from Nike. James signed a variety of deals including Coca-Cola for their Sprite and PowerAde brands (McCarthy, 2003). Bubblicious gum also signed James to a multiyear contract citing James' long-time loyalty and use of the chewing gum.

Endorsement earnings are not restricted to the US market. The leading endorser in world motor sports is Michael Schumacher. The six-time Formula 1 driving champion reportedly earns a salary of US$48 million from Ferrari and another US$96 million from endorsements and merchandising (Lomas, 2004). It may be of interest to note that Formula 1 drivers own the sponsorship rights to their helmet, whereas the team owner has the rights to signage on the car and the driver's uniform. Unfortunately for the driver trying to leverage a substantial fee, research shows that only 6% of the exposure value comes from the driver's helmet. Thirty-three percent comes from the car and 24% comes from the driver's suit.

Endorsement opportunities are not limited to traditional sports. Six-time Tour De France champion Lance Armstrong's endorsement earnings totaled US$16 million annually and ranged from Trek bicycles and Coke to Subaru motorcars. So called Extreme Sports like snowboarding and motor-cross also present athletes with endorsements. Skateboarder Tony Hawk is reported to have earnings of more than US$10 million from his products but most significantly from his Pro Skater video game. In 2003, it was the #1 sports video game and #3 seller of all video games. Hawk obtained is fame principally through the X-Games, an event developed by US sports network ESPN and broadcast in 145 different countries.

Controversies

Controversies also erupted during the 1992 Olympic Games, when the USA men's basketball team won the gold medal. Several members of the "Dream Team" had endorsement contracts with Nike, yet Reebok had supplied the US Olympic Committee with its presentation uniforms. Just prior to the medal ceremony, some team members refused to display the Reebok logo during the medal presentations. A compromise was reached wherein players who objected could open the collars of their uniform to cover the logo or drape a US flag over the offending logo. For 1998, the USOC established new, more restrictive, guidelines for logos on team apparel and revised their athlete-participation agreement. The code of conduct for the Athens 2004 Games does not allow athletes to "conceal or cover up and USOC sponsor, supplier, or licensee brand of other identification" (Lombardo, 2004, p. 5). The absurdity of this type of situation was further underscored when Los Angeles Laker Shaquille O'Neal appeared in a *Sports Illustrated* photo with tape over a sponsor's logo on his team warm-up jacket because it conflicted with his shoe sponsor.

There are issues regarding the use of women as endorsers and their use as sex objects. It has been reported that "some elite beach female volleyballers have had their breasts enlarged and other over-train their stomach muscles in an effort to obtain the hard, rippled abdomen now touted by the fitness industry as the sexy in-look for women. The intent for both of these body-sculpturing strategies is to use sex appeal to attract an audience to the contests and to attract commercial sponsorship and endorsement contracts" (Brooks, 2001, p. 1). At the center of the controversy is tennis player Anna Kournikova. While near the top of women's tennis she was able to secure endorsements from a variety of companies, but in the process she began focusing more on her modeling career than tennis and dropped out of the world rankings. Her endorsements, however, continued to rise, based predominately on her attractiveness. Her reported earnings exceed $15 million per year. One of her endorsements was for British company Berlei's Shock Absorber Multiway Sports Bra (number one seller in Britain) and featured the ad line "only the ball should bounce" (McCarthy, 2003). This clearly crossed the line from athleticism to sexism. Fink, Kensicki, Fitzgerald, and Brett (2004) referred to this type of endorsement as hyper-sexualized. In their research, they investigated whether a woman's attractiveness or expertise would more effectively influence consumers. Their findings showed that expertise was more effective in establishing a fit between the athlete and the product and therefore would better influence consumers. In related research, Brooks (2001, p. 3) noted "marketers using a sexual appeal approach find it very difficult to determine how consumers will interpret this type of message." Brooks contends that "promoting sport by using the female players as a sexual impulse stimulus may not be a profitable long-term course for either the sport or for the sponsors" (p. 8).

Overall, women make considerably less than their male counterparts in sport endorsements. The highest women's individual endorsement contract to date was secured by tennis player Venus Williams who signed a 5-year, US$40 million deal with Reebok in 2000. Her sister, Serena signed an agreement with Nike in 2003 for a total of US$60 million over 8 years. Both sisters average about $15 million per year in off-court earnings. Another leader in endorsement earnings is golf star Annika Sorenstam, who reportedly made over US$10 million in 2003 endorsement earnings (Gatlin, 2003). Serena Williams and Sorenstam were voted as the top two (respectively) marketable women in 2003, followed by Mia Hamm, Venus Williams and Lisa Leslie. Anna Kournikova was sixth on the list (Glase, 2003).

Almost all sports organizations have so-called "billboard" rules, regulating the size of sponsor logos that appear on uniforms. The NCAA, the NFL, the NBA, MLB and the NHL all have such legislation. The IOC as does as well, but a lesson was learned by the IOC at the 1988 Seoul Olympics. It limited the size of logos on swimming touch pads, starting blocks and timing devices, but not the number of logos. Consequently, timing sponsor Seiko literally covered its equipment with tiny little logos. There was also a dispute over tattoos as advertising. In 2001, boxer Bernard Hopkins enter the ring with a corporate logo (GoldenPalace.com) tattoo on his back. Although it was not prohibited in the existing rules, the Nevada State Athletic Commission acted quickly to enact legislation to prohibit such actions in the future. In another incident, NBA player Rasheed Wallace entertained an offer from a candy company to place a temporary tattoo on his bicep. Wallace declined the offer, but NBA commissioner David Stern commented that "although NBA rules did not specifically prohibit body billboards, ... its rules and restrictions with respect to both player endorsements and commercial logos on uniforms would enable the league to prevent Wallace from wearing a temporary tattoo featuring a corporate logo" (McKelvey, 2003, p. 3).

The dispute over logos has not been confined to team sports. During the 1998 US Open (tennis), Venus Williams was fined $100 by the WTA for refusing to wear the Corel WTA Tour patch on her clothing. Williams cited her Reebok contract language which "prohibited any other logo" on her dress (Kaplan, 1998, p. 9). Interestingly, the WTA rules allowed an exemption for Nike. Williams threatened to sue, but ultimately acquiesced. Reebok stayed above the fray saying that Williams could do whatever she wanted to do (Kaplan, 1998). Similarly, in 2002 Jennifer Capriati wore a Ferrari logo on the front of her shirt in "blatant disregard" for WTA rules. As of July 2003, the ATP relaxed its restrictions on logos. The previous rule was that a player could not wear a non-apparel logo on the front of a shirt. (i.e., VISA). If a player had a Nike logo on the front the player had to put the ATP logo on the back. The modification to the rule allowed non-apparel logos and apparel logos and did not require the ATP logo. However, the four Grand Slam events to date still prohibit non-apparel logos on player shirts. McKelvey noted that these instances "illustrate a growing tension between the desire and the need of sport organizations to regulate and control their business and players, versus the individual freedoms of players, particularly with respect to their pursuit of commercial endorsements" (McKelvey, 2003, p. 3).

So contentious is the issue of control that litigation was initiated against the NCAA over the issue. In 1998, adidas filed suit against the NCAA because it restricted advertising logos by manufacturers, yet allowed its own logos, sport conferences and football bowl sponsors' logos to exceed the standards. In 2004, several jockeys went to court to and won the right to sell advertising on their silks. "I know that there are people who fear that jockeys will now look like logo-covered NASCAR drivers, ruining the majesty and tradition of the Run for the Roses. But if tradition-rich events like the Masters can survive Tiger Woods and the Nike hype machine, the Sport of Kings can withstand a few dollars trickling down to the peasants" (Isidore, 2004b). Jockeys, unless they finish in the top three, can go home with as little $56 for a race.

Agents and Agencies

Marketing agents are typically the individuals responsible for assisting athletes in obtaining sponsorships and product endorsements. However, many athletes have other related business and marketing needs. These could include personal appearances and speaking engagements, appearances in screen, television, print advertising, and investment management. Few individual agents could competently furnish all of the services cited above. Therefore, several companies have been established to offer athletes a package of services from experts in each area.

The leaders in the athlete representation field are SFX Entertainment and the International Management Group (IMG). These firms have well-earned professional reputations and represent some of the top athletes in the world. In 1997, SFX Entertainment became one of the most successful agencies through their acquisition of smaller agencies that represented an array of properties in the sport and entertainment field. They managed 110 venues and over 20,000 events. To enhance their sport properties, they purchased FAME (Falk Associates Management Enterprises), headed by David Falk (Michael Jordan's long-standing agent), as well as other successful properties such as The Marquee Group. Falk currently heads SFX's Sport Group which produced $180 million of SFX's $884 million in revenues. Their services include athlete representation marketing, event management, television programming and production (Ferrel, 1999).

IMG is the second largest of these firms with 77 offices in 38 different countries; in contrast, Advantage International has 16 offices worldwide. IMG not only represents athletes, provides business and marketing services, but it owns and produces several major international sporting events. Globally, there are other firms engaged in the business as well. The industry is not, however, free from problems.

There exists a formidable amount of criticism about potential conflicts of interest when an agency both owns the event and represents the players. In relation to antitrust aspects and these immense, broad-based agencies, SFX Entertainment CEO, Mike Ferrel commented, "We've had conversations with the Department of Justice. We have no conversations that are ongoing" (Ferrel, 1999, p. 30.). Nike also found itself in a similar situation with its corporate-owned athlete representation division. "You can only represent one person at the table without being accused of having your hands in too many pockets" (Bernstein, 1998, p. 19). One has to wonder if Nike could really leverage the greatest amount of money from an array of shoe companies for a player it represents. To enable the reader to get a more thorough understanding of agent representation, a sample agent-athlete contract for management has been included at the end of this chapter.

Agent fees can run as high as 5-15% on marketing and endorsement projects. However, the professional league (NBA, WNBA, MLB, NFL, NHL) players' associations in the US generally restrict agent fees on playing contracts to 3%. The key question to be asked is on what monies the percentage of fees are calculated and if the money is paid on salary actually paid to the player or the total value of the negotiated contract.

In fairness to sports agents, most of them do safeguard the best interests of their players. In fact, they often are more knowledgeable about the player's worth than the player may be and they have a working knowledge of the types of performance provisions that can go into a player's contract. In the final analysis, agents will be better at negotiating the contract than the athlete.

Trends

Although there is some sentiment that the famous players, both team and individual, are effective as product endorsers and corporate spokespersons, there are some indicators the times may be changing. Many of the leading sport shoe manufacturers downsized their endorsement contracts in the late 1990s. For example, in 1995 Reebok had 130 NBA players under endorsement contracts, but reduced the number to 10 in 1998 (Lombardo, 1998). While reports suggest the reduction was based on changes in company revenues, some suggested that "brat-like" attitudes and consumer indifference were more likely the cause. Similarly, Nike cut endorsement spending considerably due to a downturn in market conditions and sales (Mullen, 1998). Notwithstanding, the fact that 50% of the 1998-99 NBA season was lost because of a labor dispute, the lockout may have saved Reebok and Nike a lot of endorsement money. This trend also reached into other sport industries. "Following the trend that saw sneaker companies slash endorsement contracts, major US golf club manufacturers suffering from sagging sales are cutting back on the number of golfers they pay to carry their clubs" (Mullen, 1998, p. 3).

Companies began to question the credibility and integrity of athlete endorsers in the 1990s. This questioning was accentuated by indiscretions and criminal acts by such personalities as Mike Tyson, Latrell Sprewell, and Kobe Bryant. Bryant was accused of sexual assault in 2003 and the fallout of sponsors was immediate. Adidas had just lost Bryant in early 2003 and Nike signed him for a reported $40 million at the end of the 2003 season. During the time he was charged with sexual assault, Coke suspended all of its Sprite ads with Kobe, and McDonalds did not renew its contract when it expired later in the year. Overall, 2003 was not a good year for professional sports, with more than 20 stars facing arrest and criminal charges. In response, many endorsement contracts now include special clauses to cover instances where a player or coach is involved in some scandal that reflects negatively on the sponsor. Some contracts reserve the right to terminate an agreement at any time if the commercial value of the endorsee is substantially impaired by the commission of any act which tends to denigrate, insult or offend the community standards of public morale and decency (Hein, 2003).

In reaction to this scenario, some corporations are turning increasingly to outstanding women athletes for their endorsement options. "Today's crop of women's sports standouts is, for the most part, more accessible than their male counterparts. They will autograph posters and spend time to motivate young fans" (Rodin, 1998, p. 34). They are also less likely to behave in immoral and unethical ways that might embarrass the company. Stone et. al. (2003, p. 101) noted, "our study suggests that endorsement opportunities for female athletes are growing and that elite female athletes may now be able to effectively compete with male athletes for some of the lucrative endorsement deals that have traditionally gone to men." The trend is reasonable clear, companies are looking for "squeaky clean" images and today's women athletes seem to fit the ticket (Gatlin, 2003)

Another reaction to what one author (Cordiner, 2002) dubbed the "Tyson Factor" has been to seek team and event sponsorships rather than individual athletes, signaling a trend for the future. Teams and events were determined to have more longevity than players and, thus, are more able to provide extended market influence. Additional support was provided through Volvo's Smart Sponsoring checklist that suggested that companies should "put money into the sport itself and events linked with it. Not in individual athletes" (Volvo and Sport Sponsorship, 1990, p. 5).

However, just to prove that events are not completely risk free, the 2002 Olympic Games came under US Justice Department investigation for offering bribes to IOC members and their families in an effort obtain the rights to host the Games. Several sponsors, including Qwest Communications, commented that they were "disappointed in the recent events, the negative press in general surrounding the Olympic movement and the 'lessening of value' of our substantial commitment" (Finley, 1998, p. 15A).

Irrespective of the problems associated with athlete endorsements, these individual sponsorship arrangements can be effective in marketing products and services in the sport industry. A worksheet for marketing an individual athlete has been included at the end of the chapter. Brooks and Harris (1998) suggested that the most effective endorsements are those that contain a high level of consistency between the image of the endorser and the product/service image. In fact, Boyd and Shank's (2004) research on the effectiveness of endorsements indicated that athletes were most effective when endorsing sports (as opposed to non-sport) products. This concept supports the contention of McDonald (1998) presented in Chapter 3 and research on the effectiveness of endorsements (Boyd and Shank, 2004) that carefully matching sponsorship and corporate personality is critical.

Best Practice

SAMPLE
Personal Financial Management Contract

This agreement is made this _____ day of _____, 20____, by and between _____, hereinafter "Player," and _____, hereinafter "Manager." In consideration of the promises made by each to the other, Player and Manager agree as follows:

1. FINANCIAL MANAGEMENT SERVICES - Manager hereby warrants and represents to Player that he holds college degrees in Business Administration and Law from accredited universities, with sufficient hours of study in Accounting and Marketing to qualify as majors in both fields, and that he has limited experience and training in investments. Player hereby retains Manager to advise, counsel, and assist Player in the management of income generated through Player's occupation as a professional athlete. Manager, serving in a fiduciary capacity, shall act in such manner as to protect the best interest of Player and assure effective representation of Player in matters directly and indirectly related to Player's financial situation. Manager shall not have authority to bind or commit Player to enter into any contract or agreement without actual execution thereof by the Player.

Manager shall provide financial management services to the Player as follows: (i) tax planning and preparation of federal and state income tax returns; (ii) assisting Player in determining a satisfactory budget of Player's income on a monthly and yearly basis; (iii) assisting Player in establishing investment goals; (iv) assisting Player in evaluating investment opportunities proposed to Player; (v) assisting Player in securing duly qualified professionals for legal, accounting, estate planning, investment, and insurance services as Player may desire or need.

In the event Manager shall be able to provide professional services set out in (v) above, he must provide said services at the normal rate charged to his clients in said area of professional expertise.

2. FINANCIAL MANAGER'S COMPENSATION - For services provided to the Player pursuant to the terms of Paragraph 1 of this Agreement, above, Player shall pay to Manager an amount that, when added to fees paid to Manager pursuant to the Agreement to represent Player in contract negotiations that was executed on _____, 20___, shall equal three per cent (3%) of Player's gross income from base salary, signing bonus, reporting bonus, and squad bonus as set forth in his Player's contract for the year in which services are performed, payable as received by the Player from his club.

3. INVESTMENT SERVICES - Manager agrees to keep Player informed of any investment opportunities which the Manager feels may be beneficial to the Player. In the event that the Manager shall secure an investment opportunity for the Player which the Player desires to acquire, he shall keep accurate statements as to

the condition of said investment, and shall report said conditions to the Player no less frequently than every three months, or, if information is not available at such intervals, immediately upon receipt of a status report from the record-keeping source of said investment.

Player may, at his discretion, empower Manager to exercise all rights of ownership with regards to the investments made by Manager on behalf of Player, by executing written documents which specifically set out the powers given to Manager by Player for such matters as collection of income, purchase of additional interests in each said investment, or sale or transfer of said investment.

4. COMPENSATION - Player shall pay to Manager a sum equal to five per cent (5%) of the appreciation in value, income received, whether ordinary or capital gain, for each investment made by Manager on behalf of Player.

For purposes of this Paragraph, investments made for Player by a qualified and licensed investment broker secured by Manager for Player shall not be considered to be made by the Manager, and Player shall not be liable for compensation to Manager for income or appreciation in value of said investments.

5. PERSONAL APPEARANCE SERVICES - Manager shall use his best efforts to assist Player in enhancing Player's public image and in assisting Player in securing personal appearances, such as, but not limited to, speaking engagements, commercial endorsements, autograph sessions, promotions, licensing arrangements, and appearances in any mass media outlet. Player shall use such efforts as are reasonably necessary to appear at said opportunities, and to improve speaking and related talents so as to provide a good public image for himself and the organization for which he is appearing.

6. COMPENSATION - For all types of public appearances opportunities secured for Player by the Manager, the Player shall pay to the Manager a sum equal to fifteen per cent (15%) of the gross income received by Player for each said appearance. For purposes of public appearance opportunities only, Manager shall be responsible for expenses incurred by him in attempting to secure said opportunities for Player, unless Player agrees in writing to reimburse Manager for expenses incurred on Player's behalf in these matters.

7. EXPENSES - Except as provided in Paragraph 6 above, Player shall reimburse Manager for all expenses that are reasonable and necessary in providing the services on Player's behalf as set out in this Agreement, upon receipt of an itemized statement of said expenses from Manager to the Player.

8. ENTIRE AGREEMENT - This Agreement sets forth the entire agreement between the parties hereto and replaces or supersedes all prior agreements between the parties related to the same subject matter. This Agreement cannot be changed orally.

9. TERM - This agreement shall remain in full force and effect for a period of one year from the date above or until the final contract negotiated by Manager for Player with a professional athletic team has expired, whichever shall last occur. However, Player and Manager shall have the right to terminate this Agreement with written notice delivered personally or by regular United States mail to the party at his last-known address, and upon the payment of all fees and expenses

due hereunder by the terminating party to the other party.

10. GOVERNING LAW - This Agreement shall be construed, interpreted and enforced according to the laws of the State of _____.

EXAMINE THIS CONTRACT CAREFULLY

BEFORE SIGNING IT

 IN WITNESS WHEREOF, the parties hereto have hereunto signed their names as hereinafter set forth.

_____   _____

AGENT   PLAYER

References

Bennett, G., Henson, R, and Zhang, J. (2002). Action sports sponsorship recognition. *Sport Marketing Quarterly*, 11 (3), 25-34.

Bernstein, A. (1998, September 29 - October 4). Working both sides of the plate. *Sports Business Journal*, 19, 28.

Boyd, T., and Shank, M. (2004). Athletes as product endorsers: The effect of gender and product relatedness. *Sport Marketing Quarterly*, 13, 2, 82-93.

Brooks, C. M. (2001, Spring). Using sex appeal as a sport promotion strategy. *Women in Sport & Physical Activity Journal, 10* (1), 1-11.

Brooks, C. M., and Harris, K. K. (1998). Celebrity athlete endorsement: An overview of the key theoretical issues. *Sport Marketing Quarterly, 7* (2), 34-44.

Cordiner, R. (2002, June-July). Boxing and sponsorship: A mismatch of a knockout combination. *International Journal of Sports Marketing and Sponsorship*, 175-181.

Ferrel, M. (1999, November 22-28). The network advantage. *Sports Business Journal*, 30-31.

Fink, J., Kensicki, L., Fitzgerald, M., and Brett, M. (2004) *Using Female Athletes as Endorsers of Events: Attractiveness Versus Expertise*. Atlanta, GA: Conference of the North American Society for Sport Management.

Finley, B. (1998, December 24) Utah bid probed by feds. *Denver Post*, p. 1A, 15A.

Gatlin, G. (2003, Dec. 31). In endorsements, youth wins. *Boston Herald*, O27.

Glase, T. (2003, September 18). Serena Williams voted most marketable female athlete. *Sports Business Daily, 6* (2), 10.

Goldman, L. (2000). Going to xtremes. *Forbes, 165* (8), 18.

Hein, K. (2003, July 14). A broken field of dreams. *Brandweek*, 15.

Isidore, C. (2004a). *Tiger's still a winner for sponsors*. Retrieved June 21 from http://www.money.cnn.com/2004/06/18/comentary-sports-biz/index.htm.

Isidore, C. (2004b). *Big win for the little guys*. Retrieved April 30 from http://www.money.cnn.com/2004/04/30/comentary/column_sportbiz/index.htm.

Kaplan, D. (1998, September 7-13). Venus patches rift with WTA. *Sports Business Journal*, 9.

Kaufman, M. (1998, May 11-17). Women take their place at the table. *Sports Business Journal*, 1, 48.

Lomas, G. (2004). *F1 stars rake in the big bucks*. Retrieved April 13 from http://0-lexis-nexis.com.source.unco.edu/universe/docuemtn?_=37ce39631be812ae

Lombardo, J. (1998, May 18-24). Reebok downsizing NBA deal. *Sports Business Journal*, 6.

Lombardo, J. (2004, July 19-25). Nike endorsers will dominate Reebok-clad US hoops team. *Sport Business Journal*, 5.

McCarthy, M. (2003, August 22). Win or lose, drawing, endorsements is key. *USA Today*, 1B.

McDonald, M. (1998). *Sport Sponsorship and the Role of Personality Matching*. Buffalo, NY: Conference of the North American Society for Sport Management.

McKelvey, M. (2003, Winter). *Commercial Branding: the final frontier or false start for athletes' use of temporary tattoos as body billboards. Journal of the Legal Aspects of Sport*. Retrieved September 3 from http://)-web.lexis-nexis.com.source.unco.edu/universe.

Mullen, L. (1998, October 5-11) Biz woes reach golfers. *Sports Business Journal*, 3.

Rodin, S. (1998, May 11-17). Shrewd marketers can share in boom. *Sports Business Journal*, 34.

Schlossberg, H. (1990, April 7). Allure of Celebrity Endorsers Starts to Fade. *Marketing News*, p. 7.

Spiegel, P. (1998, December 14). Heir Gordon. *Forbes*,188-197.

Stone, G., Joseph, M, and Jones, M. (2003). An exploratory study on the use of sport celebrities in advertising: a content analysis. *Sport Marketing Quarterly, 12* (2), 94-102.

Veltri, F. (1996). *Recognition of Athlete-Endorsed Products*. Frederickton, NB: Conference of the North American Society for Sport Management.

Volvo and Sport Sponsorship. (1990, January 29). *Special Events Reports*, pp. 4-5.

Individual Athlete Sponsorship Worksheets

The worksheets provide a guide for you in developing various sections of a sponsorship plan. The following sheets cover areas that must be addressed when attempting to secure endorsements for individual athletes. Complete these worksheets as a preparatory step in the creation of a sponsorship plan.

Specify the image, personal likes and dislikes, as well as speaking abilities of your athlete.

_____

_____

_____

_____

_____

_____

_____

_____

_____

Prepare a list of the products currently used by your athlete.

_____

_____

_____

_____

Identify possible VIK opportunities

_____

_____

_____

_____

_____

Report the specific sport-imposed time constraints that would affect endorsement appearances.

_____

_____

_____

_____

_____

Calculate the relative value of your athlete compared to other athletes.

_____

_____

_____

_____

_____

Brainstorm tentative corporations that could be targeted for consideration.

_____

_____

_____

_____

_____

Research the most likely corporations for approach.

_____

_____

_____

_____

_____

Assemble an *athlete package* including a cover letter, athlete bio, photographs, previous endorsements, and family background.

_____

_____

_____

_____

Establish a calendar for presenting or mailing packages to potential corporations and set your allowable response timeline.

_____

_____

_____

_____

Create a checklist to track the results of your efforts.

_____

_____

_____

_____

Chapter Six

Financial Implications

Introduction

The finances involved in sports sponsorships are staggering. As mentioned in the first chapter of this workbook, worldwide spending on sponsorship was estimated to be $28 billion in 2004. It's also important to remember that not all sponsorship arrangements involve the exchange of cash. Successful sponsorships often involve trading goods and services that a corporation controls and the sport organization may need. This has generally been termed value-in-kind (VIK) and on average 40% of all sponsorship agreements encompass at least some provision involving the supply of products and services. Several examples have been presented throughout this workbook. Colleges and universities trade sponsorship and signage for uniforms and shoes, the Olympics accepts computers and data processing in return for sponsorship, and many road races accept energy drinks in return for on-course signage. It is important, however, to heed the words of Mike Mushett, an executive with the 1996 Paralympic Games, "You can't meet payroll with M&M's and Coke" (Mushett, 1995).

What sponsors are looking for is a positive return on their investments. Dannon calculated a positive return on their sponsorship of the Dannon Duathlon Championship Series. Partnering with local grocery stores in each of the eight yearly events, Dannon was able to generate $750,000 from their $250,00 investment (Dannon sponsorship, 2003). Ukman (2004) also provided a breakout of calculating ROI for a boat show that is included at the end of this chapter as a Best Practice.

Details of the sponsorship agreement between adidas and the Tampa Bay Buccaneers may provide insight to the seldom-seen financial side of sponsorships (Friedman, 1999, p. 36.) The Tampa Bay Buccaneers put together sponsorship packages for their new stadium for adidas. Through a five-year, $1.7 million agreement, adidas agreed to provide $4.4 million in products and $675,000 for community outreach programs. The package included, among other items 1) two 22-by-28 foot trivision panels on each scoreboard, 2) one corporate identification (five feet high) above the lower suite level, 3) inclusion of the corporate logo in one 16-by-40 foot themed mural in the main stadium concourse, 4) signs at six novelty stands, 5) one sponsor identification on the score board per quarter of play, 6) two full-page advertisements in NFL Insider, 7) periodic mention in the Buccaneers newsletter, 8) ability to place promotional flyers in stadium cup holders for each game, 9) presence on team's Internet home page, 10) one 16-person luxury suite, 11) 70 season tickets for all home games (10 in club section and 60 in preferred general admission seating sections), 12) 16 tickets for the 2001 Super Bowl, 13) four parking passes, 14) one catered tailgate party for 100 guests, 15) VIP day for 20 guests at one practice session during the season, 16) one away game trip per season for four guests (Freidman, 1999). In this package, no elements were priced individually but rather bundled together with a total price for all components.

Pricing Sponsorships

The first thing the sport marketer needs to know about pricing a sponsorship is that nobody cares how much money your sport organization needs. They only care about the value that they can get from the partnership. Several different approaches to sponsorship pricing have been utilized extensively in the industry. Brooks (1994) outlined the three most often used methods for sponsorship pricing:

1. "Cost-plus" method—In this technique you calculate the actual expenses incurred in providing the sponsorship package plus a desired profit for the organization. Costs include all items: tickets, parking, dinners, souvenirs, and signage. This method has been used effectively by the USOC to price the sponsorship packages for the United States Olympic Congress. In using this method, be sure to include the labor costs associated with the production of the above elements. In this manner, you will be able to demonstrate the true profits to senior management.

2. "Competitive market" strategy—As with any product pricing strategy, you must be competitive with alternative sponsorship options. The problem is trying to discover their price. In the sponsorship business it is difficult to know the pricing structure of competitors' packages. One of the best ways is to read prominent trade publications. The leading publication on sport sponsorship is the *IEG Sponsorship Report*. This biweekly newsletter covers all of the major activity in the sponsorship industry and includes interviews with industry leaders. For example, the newsletter tracks worldwide spending and reports trends in North America as well as around the globe. Another noteworthy publication is the *Sports Business Journal*. While this weekly publication does not focus solely on sport sponsorship, it does present a variety of articles on the topic. The *IEG Sponsorship Report* systematically lists the prices of all major sponsorship signing on a quarterly basis.

3. "Relative value" method—This approach to pricing is based on the market value of each sponsorship component. For example, if you are including souvenir program ads in your sponsorship package you could compare this component to the price and effectiveness of ads in the newspaper. Scoreboard signage could be valued against the cost of billboards, and PA announcements could be equated with radio advertising. You will need to ascertain if the comparison is legitimate and if the same impact is achieved. This can be accomplished through a review of the cost per thousand (CPM—M representing the Roman numeral for 1000). Even if your CPM turns out to be higher, you might argue that your audience is a better demographic match than a mass media ad. It has been reported that event-based media elements are somewhat less effective than a direct advertising message. Their suggested value is about 20% of the media cost, but, if the events provided actual advertising spots during event TV broadcasts and legitimate advertising space from a media sponsor, the value would be equal to the full rate offered to other advertisers (Stotlar, 2001; Ukman, 2004).

In an effort to help event owners justify return on investment to sponsors, one company, Joyce Julius and Associates has been providing support data for more than ten years. Their concept was to tabulate the total time that a sponsor's logo appeared on TV coverage of major events, then provide an exposure value based on the cost of airing a 30-second commercial during the same period. For example, data from the 2003 NASCAR series indicated that Chevrolet became the first sponsor to break the $200 million mark in exposure value. Chevy logos were seen on screen for a total of 15 hours and enjoyed 450 sponsor mentions. Placement of the logos is also critical. It can't be argued that the best place to be on NASCAR is the hood and rear quarter panel. However, even companies like 3M generated $8 million in exposure value from a fender decal. Data from the 2004 bowl games showed logo placement on the 20-yardline outperformed midfield logos 4-to-1 (Joyce Julius, 2004a). Even the controversial logos on jockeys during the 2004 Triple Crown races produced significant values. The sponsors' logo presence (shirt, hat, pant legs) on Stewart Elliott, jockey for Smarty Jones, enabled the sponsor to earn $834,160 as a result of 1:31 of clear, in-focus time (Joyce Julius, 2004b).

In 2004 Nielson Sports was created to compete with Joyce Julius. They followed the same process but extended the concept to cover on screen logos and signage that appeared in sports news broadcasts like ESPN's Sport Center. Some have argued that the same advertising message is not delivered in on-screen logo presence as can be presented in a 30-second ad. However, that rationale fails if one accounts for "channel surfers" and TiVo users who don't watch the commercials, but are exposed to in-event messages. Perhaps a smart strategy is to use a ratio in assessing the value of such exposure. IEG suggests that sponsors apply a 1 - 5 ratio in decreasing the value for on-screen logo appearance versus the actual cost of the commercial (Ukman, 2004).

Sponsors have also been known to use all of these price valuation methods for analyzing proposed sponsorship packages. NationsBank's sport and event marketing vice president said, "When I receive a proposal, I do a payout analysis, putting dollars against each benefit the property is offering" (Goldberg, 1998, p. 29).

Collateral Support

To sufficiently support a sport sponsorship, corporations must be willing to spend additional dollars promoting their involvement. Estimates vary among corporations on how much additional spending will be required to increase visibility of the sponsorship and to activate consumers. The general rule is that a sponsor must be willing to spend an amount at least equal to the rights fee of their sponsorship to leverage the effect. Nextel's $45 million per year title sponsorship of NASCAR includes a commitment form the sponsors to spend a like amount on marketing the relationship (Rovell, 2004). Coca-Cola estimates its ratio as 5 -1, spending $5.00 on promotions and advertising for every $1.00 it spends on sponsorship fees. AT&T spent six times the cost of their sponsorship to make their sponsorships "known to employees and felt by customers" (Ukman, 1998, p. 2). Other authorities recommend that, at a minimum, sponsors spend an amount at least equal to the sponsorship fee for promotion and leveraging (Bernstein, 1998; Stotlar, 2001). A sponsorship alone, without collateral support, will rarely produce the desired results. The partnership must be leveraged through all of the sponsor's and the organization's assets.

Small Budget Sponsorships

In most small companies or divisions, the budget doesn't include a spare $700,000 to get involved in high priced sport sponsorships. However, several companies have been successful in low budget sponsorships that have produced good results. Even at the Olympic level, sponsors can get in for a modest amount of money. By sponsoring US Speed Skating for the 2002 Winter Olympic games uniform sponsors were able to have their logo appear on the cover of *Sports Illustrated* when Casey Fitzrandolf won a gold medal in the 500m. A full-page color ad in *Sports Illustrated* costs over $200,000 but there is no price for the cover. In another example, Bavarian Coachworks, a company specializing in customized Porsches, spent only $40,000 to get prime ad placement on a racecar entered in 17 events. The shop owner credited the ad with increasing his business 60-70%, many times above the cost of the sponsorship. Local auto racing can be even cheaper; some drivers will almost give ad space away just so they can look like "real" sponsored racers.

At some point, the sport marketer has to ask for money from the sponsor (more detail on specific strategies will be presented in Chapter 8). It's much easier if the marketer has presented the financial benefits in a clear and precise manner. The sport marketer provides a service, a true benefit that can be measured in dollars, and is not asking for a charity handout. One major problem occurs when the "money is put on the table." If a sponsor offers $3,000 for a $10,000 package, the sport marketer has to walk away. A good package will stand on its own merit. With this business approach and attitude, a positive response is likely. An effective sport marketer has the data to show that sport sponsorship doesn't cost; it pays.

Best Practice

The following example was constructed by IEG (Ukman, 2004, p. 4) as a best practice in calculating return on sponsorship. The scenario details the results for an automotive manufacturer's $50,000 sponsorship of a boat show where the primary objective was to increase sport utility vehicle (SUV) sales.

Boat show attendance	= 40,000
Attendees who visited booth and pickup test drive offer	= 14,000
Booth visitors who visited dealer for a test drive (7%)	= 980
Test drivers who purchased within 12 mo. period (12%)	= 118
Average profit per vehicle	= $2,000
Gross profit from sponsorship	= $236,000
Rights fees	- $50,000
Production and promotion costs	- $50,000
Net profit	= $136,000
Return on investment	= 136%

References

Bernstein, A. (1998, June 22-28). Leagues hit it big in gold rush. *Sports Business Journal,* 19, 32.

Dannon sponsorship stirs 3-to-1 return. (2003). *IEG Sponsorship Report, 22* (21), 1-2.

Freidman, A. (1999, March - April 4). Rare glimpse at the selling of a stadium. *Sports Business Journal,* 36-37.

Goldberg, R. (1998, June 22-28). Toughest task: Measuring results. *Sports Business Journal,* 29.

Joyce Julius & Associates (2004). *Second Look.* Retrieved February 19 from http://www.joyce-julius.com/newletter/a-second-look-feb-2004.htm

Joyce Julius & Associates (2004a). *Second Look.* Retrieved August 3 from http://www.joycejulius.com/newletter/a-second-look-aug-2004.htm

Mushett, M. (1995). *Sponsorship and the Paralympic Games. Atlanta:* Conference of the North American Society for Sport Management.

Rovell, D. (2004). *Sports Biz.* Retrieved Feb 23 from http://sports.espn.go.com/espn/sportbusiness/news/story?id=174215.

Stotlar, D. K. (2001). *Developing Successful Sport Marketing Plans, 1st ed.* Morgantown, WV, Fitness Information Technology.

Ukman, L. (1998, March 20). Assertions. *IEG Sport Sponsorship Report.* 2.

Ukman, L. (2004). *Return on Sponsorship.* Chicago: International Events Group.

Financial Worksheets

The worksheets provide a guide for you in developing various sections of a sponsorship plan. The following sheets cover the financial aspects of pricing a sponsorship. Complete these worksheets as a preparatory step in the creation of a sponsorship plan.

Calculate a price for your sponsorship using the cost-plus method

_____

_____

_____

_____

_____

_____

_____

_____

_____

Compare the market value of similar sponsorships with your cost-plus calculations above and evaluate the need for any adjustments in pricing your sponsorship.

_____

_____

_____

_____

_____

_____

_____

_____

_____

_____

Complete a relative value calculation by examining the media and retail tie-in portions of your sponsorship (if applicable) and evaluate the need for any adjustments in pricing your sponsorship.

_____

_____

_____

_____

_____

_____

_____

_____

Examine the needs that your organization may have for sponsor products or services and prepare a list of possible VIK contributions and their appropriate value.

_____

_____

_____

_____

_____

_____

_____

_____

_____

_____

_____

Chapter Seven

Developing Successful Sport Sponsorship Proposals

Chapter Outline

Introduction

This chapter will present an overview and a conceptual model for development of sport sponsorship proposals derived from field-based applications. Specific examples and procedures will be examined and presented for you to use as models in building sponsorships for your sport organization.

Sport has proven revenue potential as a marketing vehicle and the sponsorship proposal is the essential element. The task of the sport manager lies in presenting a proposal that specifically identifies sponsors benefits and needs discussed in Chapter 3. However, it cannot be stressed enough that corporations are looking for flexibility, not set bundles of components. One corporate executive commented, "Most properties package what they need to sell without thinking what has value for their partners" (Goldberg, 1998, p. 29). The preferable strategy carefully examines each sponsor and uncovers the requisite needs for each potential sponsor.

One of the best sources to access information on the inside operations of companies sponsoring sport events is *IEG Sponsorship Report* referenced earlier in the workbook. This Chicago-based biweekly publication from the International Events Group (IEG) provides detailed analyses of sponsorship packages and the attendant framework. They also frequently list requests for sponsorship proposals from a variety of corporations.

Getting information about potential sponsors is essential. If the company is a publicly traded company, it is required to file annual report with the Securities and Exchange Commission. Annual reports filed with the SEC (Securities and Exchange Commission) can also be accessed through the SEC's web site (www.sec.gov) and through Public Register's Annual Report Service (www.prars.com). Each of these sources can provide valuable data for use in structuring a sponsorship proposal.

In an effort to deal with an increasing number of proposals, many corporations are moving to online submission of sponsorship proposals. To this end, some corporations have specific criteria for proposals. A sample of a format modified from several online sites is provided below. Other corporations will consider any reasonable format devised by the event or property owner. In addition, excerpts and sample wording from authentic sponsorship proposals have been included at the end of the chapter in Best Practice.

The level of sophistication has increased with the maturity of the industry in the last ten years. Accordingly, few boilerplate sponsorship proposals are effective. In an effort to save time, some sport properties attempt to create a boilerplate proposal to distribute to multiple sponsors. These boilerplates usually contain the entire inventory the organization has collected to package in their sponsorship, but little attention is given to molding the package to the targeted corporation. A simple cut-and-paste approach is taken to generate as many proposals as possible. Lauletta (Director of Sports and Event Marketing for Miller Brewing Company) said, "I still receive proposals with Coors and Heineken name in place of Miller, and it always amazes me how lazy someone can be" (Lauletta, 2003, p. 8). Recipients easily expose this generic approach and the proposal is most likely discarded.

Sponsorship Submission Format Model

Name of the Event

Event Management Contact
- Name
- Title
- Address
- Phone
- FAX
- Email

Event Management Experience

Event Location(s)

Venue

Description of the Event

Image Match and Integration

Number of Events
- One time Only
- Series of Events

Duration of the Event
- Proposed Date(s)

Audience Size

Audience Demographics
- Gender Profile

Percentage in Age Groups
- Percentage in Income Brackets
- Ethnicity Profile
- Lifestyle Characteristics (AOI)

Media Profile (specify coverage under contract, historical data, or projected coverage)
- TV
- Newspaper
- Radio

Promotional Plan (specify coverage type, length, units, frequency, production details, and sponsors access)
- TV
- Newspaper
- Radio
- Web Site
- Direct Mail
- Database
- PR Events
- Live Marketing Events

Level of Sponsorship (title, presenting, supplier, etc.)

Sponsorship Category, Parameters and Exclusivity

Former Sponsors (list company, category, level, and year)

Existing & Proposed Sponsors (list company(s), category, and level; indicate if under contract or proposed)

Sponsorable Components & Benefits
- Signage
- Venue Messaging
- Tag to Media Advertising
- Hospitality (suites, tickets, passes, parking, food and beverage)
- Pre-Event Activities
- In-Event Activities
- On-site Product Trial
- On-Site Display
- On-site Product Sales
- Ceremonies
- Celebrity/Athlete/VIP Access or Appearance
- Value-in-Kind (VIK) Opportunities
- Cross-promotion opportunities
- Licensing
- Post-Event Activities
- Other

Identified Measures for Evaluation Report

Rationale (why and how each benefit is an appropriate fit to the sponsor)

Proposed Budget and Value of Benefits

In putting together a sponsorship proposal, Ukman (1995) suggested several attributes that should be addressed in a quality sponsorship proposal. She emphasizes that the proposal should promote "benefits," not "package features." Company executives are looking for promotional platforms that can effectively produce quantifiable advantages for the company. Therefore, the focus of the proposal should be on the sponsor's needs, not the property's. Ukman indicated that too often the proposal spends an inordinate amount of space detailing why the organization needs the money or how important it is to stage the event.

"The successful proposal is tailored to the sponsor's business category. Boilerplate proposals do not work" (Ukman, 1995, p. 2). As discussed in Chapter 3, specific attributes of a proposal may meet the image needs of one company, but another company may need product sampling. The sport marketer should work hard to establish a pre-proposal meeting in an effort to determine the specific needs of their prospects. They must do their homework and have a high level of understanding about the potential sponsor in order to actively participate in a discussion of their needs. Only then can an effective sponsorship proposal be developed. The proposal should also explain how the benefits can be leveraged through the sponsor's existing marketing programs to achieve extended impact. Finally, the best proposals communicate the advantages of alliances and strategic partnerships that will ultimately provide greater utility than either party could accomplish separately (Ukman, 1995).

Sponsorship Description

The first step in developing an outstanding sponsorship proposal is the description of the event or property offered by the organization. This includes the history, years of organizational operation, and structure of the sport enterprise. Major corporations want to know the kind of organization with which they are getting involved. According to New York-based Sports Summit, "If we are going to sponsor an event, I want to see the financial history of the people putting things together. How much can they cover? Is this event really going to come off? I know this sounds stupid, but too many people never ask that question. Those are the ones that get burned" (Macnow, 1989, p. 39).

Proposal Objectives and Match to Sponsor Needs

It has been previously pointed out that a match must be made between corporate objectives and the opportunities available through the sponsorship arrangement. Therefore, the objectives of the proposal must be clearly presented in relation to how the sponsorship will produce benefits for the sponsor. Specific objectives must be delineated regarding target market demographics, psychographics, image opportunities, awareness strategies, market share increases, and business-to-business relationships.

Just as marketing practices have changed from a product orientation to a market orientation, sponsorships have changed as well. In the early days of sponsorship, properties would put together "Gold, Silver and Bronze" style packages and offer them to potential sponsors. Those days have long ago passed and the need for flexibility and customization is essential. All too often properties are intent on selling their inventory of sponsorable components, rather presenting options to a potential sponsor that they need. Respondents in Seaver's 2004 corporate survey advised marketers to align sponsorship proposals to meet the business objectives of prospective sponsors. Attention to these factors can result in a longstanding sponsorship association.

Sponsorable Components

The individual components of sponsorship should be presented to the sponsor in detail. Every available activity or event planned should be described, including the corporate opportunities available within each activity or event. These should be linked to standard business practices that have been proven to produce results. These results should be clearly tied to actionable components of the sponsorship. For example, most corporations have a positioning strategy in place. A proposal should describe how the features of the sponsorship could assist with solidifying the corporate position in the mind of the consumer.

A good place to start is to reexamine the needs for sponsors presented in Chapter 3. When comparing what sponsors want, the sport marketer will need to conduct an audit of the benefits that the organization has to offer. There are of course the natural elements surrounding the sport organization. Items like stadium signage, title of an event or activity and advertising linked the organization's communication outlets (game/event program ads, TV, newspapers, web sites, etc.). However, with a little creativity, features like a newsletter (don't have one, create one) and access to a customer database (don't have one, create one) can really pull the sponsor into a sport organization, creating a true partnership. Sport properties also have a great opportunity to assist with product displays and product sampling. As noted in the US Swimming sponsorship by a sunscreen product, the manufacturer wanted to get its product into the hands of its target market. In another case, auto dealers were able to capitalize on grassy areas of the football stadium for vehicle display during their prime new model introduction period, with no added costs for the organization, "$0." Other assets like hospitality, inclusion in PR events and permission to co-promote with your logo are great additions to a sport marketer's inventory.

One of the best features about sport is that we have an inventory that cannot be duplicated by many other industries. Yes, sponsors can buy other television exposure, and they can buy ads in newspapers and magazines, but they can't buy access to players and coaches or behind the scenes tours in sport venues. In 2004, one of the sponsors (an auto dealership) of the Denver Grand Prix was able to offer a lap around the racecourse for any customer who bought a new vehicle during the promotional period. This is a benefit that was created especially for this sponsor. It was creative and effective and had no added sponsorship costs.

Sports teams also have the benefit of providing access to "Game Used" items like game-worn jerseys and game balls for sponsors. While there is a cost related to providing these items, that cost easily can be offset through the price of the sponsorship. These special benefits are an important part of a sport marketer's inventory. They create meaning for the fans and help transfer the emotion from the sport to the sponsor. Also, when a sport marketer combines sponsorable components, they must truly differentiate the components falling under higher levels of sponsorship from those in lower categories. The differentiating factors for components of a $100,000 sponsorship should be more than just twice as many stadium signs as the $50,000 deal.

It is also essential that the responsibility for development of each aspect be clarified. If corporate hospitality is a primary feature of the proposal, it must be verified who will provide the catering. Typically, the event or property provides the facility and arranges the dialog with approved caterers. Ultimately, it is the sponsor who selects the menu and finalizes the service protocol and details.

Pricing

The presentation of cost estimates has been an area where many sports organizations have encountered difficulties. Pricing can be prepared for either an entire proposal or for specific options within the proposal. For most sponsors, flexibility is the key.

The most important step in pricing is making an accurate valuation. Therefore, the pricing methods presented in Chapter 6 are critical. Each potential sponsor is engaged in other marketing activities, each of which has a price and value. The sport manager must study and prepare data that demonstrate the benefits of sport sponsorship in terms the corporation can understand. It is also important to remember that industry experts estimate (noted in Chapter 6) that an incremental commitment on the part of the sponsor to integrate the sponsorship with their existing marketing functions can range from an additional 100-500% of the sponsorship cost.

One aspect of sport sponsorship that has been difficult to foresee for many managers is that often corporations would rather deal with large projects than be victimized by a multitude of small ones (Fewer, Bigger, Better as discussed in Chapter 1). One of Volvo's specific recommendations for sport sponsorship is that high dollar deals are more profitable and less work that numerous small ventures (Volvo and Sport Sponsorship, 1990). Therefore, it is important to offer the company several options in their sponsorship agreement, ranging from exclusive ownership of all events and opportunities to smaller and less expensive options such as value-in-kind (VIK) provisions or associated advertising.

Preparation of the Proposal

There has been some debate regarding the actual appearance of the sponsorship proposal. Some practitioners believe that a quality proposal should have the logo of the sport entity and the sponsor's logo prominently displayed on the cover of the proposal. However, others have cautioned that sponsors may react negatively if their corporate logo was used without permission, leading them to question the ethical behavior of the organization. No clear-cut model exists, but a conservative approach would support a professionally prepared proposal without the sponsor's logo. If you are able to arrange a pre-proposal meeting, permission to use their logo may be secured. Another issue arises in the quality of the printing used for the proposal materials. Some authorities have suggested that organizations should prepare the highest quality materials that they can afford. This would include five-color glossy brochures detailing all of the benefits. On the other hand, some sport marketers believe that the material should be of a more moderate quality to leave the impression that the organization is not frivolous in its spending. The author supports producing the highest quality possible and securing VIK when available to obtain the materials.

The model presented above and the examples shown at the end of the chapter have been derived from existing sponsorship proposals and agreements and can provide sport marketers with the skills necessary to succeed in the exciting world of sponsorship.

Best Practice

*California Angels Partnership Opportunities
(Excerpts Depicting Selected Sponsorship Plan Elements)*

Event Management

"The Anaheim Angels are backed by the leaders in quality family entertainment: The Walt Disney Company."

"Our Sponsorship Services Department will thoroughly coordinate your every need."

Image

"Best of all, Angel fans and other guests will associate your business with the high quality, total sports and entertainment experience that is provided by the California Angels."

"Sponsors can be assured that their message will be favorably associated with the upscale, positive experience presented at every game."

Signage/Exposure

"If you want to see your company's name in lights, then you'll want to check out the array of signage opportunities that exist at the newly renovated Edison International Field of Anaheim. From prominent display on the scoreboard to fence signage, concourse and TV rotational advertising, and JumboTron commercials and features, millions of potential customers will be exposed to your company's products."

Integrated Communications

"If television is your medium, you'll be pleased to know that 51 of Anaheim Angels' home and road games are televised. In-game features, 30 second commercials, and opening and closing billboards are available to reinforce your message."

"Our Angels Halo Insider Magazine game programs are an outstanding place for sponsors to be noticed. More than 150,000 Halo Insider game programs are distributed each season."

Demographic Profile (Anaheim Angels Season Ticket Holder Profile)
Gender: 79% Male, 18% Female, 3% Did Not Respond
Income: 2%   Less than $25,000
                    11% $25,000-$49,999
                    16% $50,000-$74,999
                    18% $75,000-$99,999

23%	$100,000-$149,999
8%	$150,000-$199,999
14%	$200,000 +
8%	Did Not Respond

Age Distribution

2%	18-24
13%	25-34
42%	35-49
27%	50-64
11%	64 +
5%	Did Not Respond

"If your company is international, keep in mind that baseball's popularity is fast-growing in such mega markets as Japan, China and South America."

Hospitality

"Corporate entertainment also takes on a new look. There's the Diamond Club, a complete entertainment experience behind home plate; as well as, deluxe dugout level suites and renovated Club level suites, where first-class service and luxury complement exciting Major League Baseball. Club suites offer one of the most exclusive and prestigious entertainment opportunities in Southern California."

"If enhancing client and employee relationships is your goal, we offer first-class hospitality opportunities."

* Sincere appreciation is extended to Tony Tavares and Kevin Dart (formerly) with the Anaheim Sports for sharing the sponsorship package information.

References

Goldberg, R. (1998, June 22-28). Toughest task: Measuring results. *Sports Business Journal*, 29.

Lauletta, S. (2003). Negotiations part one: Executives outline approach to say no to a prospective sponsor. *Team Marketing Report*, 15, (4), 8.

Macnow, G. (1989, September). Sports tie-ins help firms score big. *IEG Sponsorship Report*.

Seaver, R. (2004). *2004 Corporate Sponsorship Survey Report*. San Diego: Seaver Marketing Group.

Ukman, L. (1995, December 4). Back to basics. *IEG Sponsorship Report*.

Volvo and Sport Sponsorship. (1990, January 29). *Special Events Reports*, pp. 4-5.

Sponsorship Proposals Worksheets

The worksheets provide a guide for developing various sections of a sponsorship proposal. The following sheets cover the creation of a sponsorship proposal. Complete these worksheets as a preparatory step in the creation of your final sponsorship proposal.

Provide an overall description of the sponsorship.

_____

_____

_____

_____

_____

_____

_____

_____

_____

Describe the organizing committee and/or management attributes of your staff.

_____

_____

_____

_____

_____

Present the similarities of demographic profiles between the sponsor's customers and your event or property.

_____

_____

_____

_____

_____

_____

Detail the match in psychographic characteristics between the sponsor's customers and your event or property.

_____

_____

_____

_____

_____

Project the anticipated or previous media coverage.

_____

_____

_____

_____

_____

List the activities included in the proposal that are designed to enhance sponsor awareness.

_____

_____

_____

_____

_____

List the opportunities included in the proposal that are designed for image building.

_____

_____

_____

_____

_____

Specify elements in the proposal designed to drive sales of sponsor products/services.

_____

_____

_____

_____

_____

Determine the potential for retailer/wholesaler tie-ins.

_____

_____

_____

_____

Articulate the sponsorship events for developing hospitality relationships.

_____

_____

_____

_____

Examine aspects of the sponsorship that could be used for employee motivation.

_____

_____

_____

_____

_____

_____

Enumerate each of the sponsorable components within the proposal.

_____

_____

_____

_____

_____

_____

_____

_____

_____

_____

_____

_____

Calculate the price of the entire sponsorship or each component in the proposal.

_____

_____

_____

_____

_____

_____

_____

_____

_____

_____

Identify each of the other current sponsors

_____

_____

_____

_____

_____

Delineate possible risks and your organization's plan to minimize those risks.

_____

_____

_____

_____

_____

Chapter Eight

Securing Sponsorship Agreements

Introduction

One of the most difficult decisions you will face after the development of your sponsorship plan will center on whom to contact at a particular company. In the industry, this is referred to as the *access or point of entry*. There has been considerable confusion over the most successful approach strategy for sponsorship acquisition. Recent research indicates that sponsorships are most often secured through the following entry channels ("IEG Survey finds," 2001, p. 5):

53%	Property approaches sponsor (cold call)
7%	Agency hired by property approaches sponsor
10%	Property Board Member contacts sponsor
25%	Sponsor contacts property directly
5%	Other

It is surprising to see the high percentage of the sponsorships that were secured through a "cold call." Cold calls result either from an actual telephone call into the sponsor's organization or from providing an unsolicited proposal through the mail. One of the biggest shock waves through the industry occurred when the $750 million Nextel-NASCAR deal started through a cold call. According to Migala (2003) for anyone selling sports sponsorships, cold calling is easily one of the most dreaded aspects of their job. Migala's advice is that before you call, you should relax and take 30 seconds to think about what you want to get across. The consensus of the sponsorship buyers he interviewed was that most sellers do not take even a few minutes to think before they call and prepare for a few of the situations that might be waiting on the other end of the line. The biggest thing is to have a real sense of why this property is a good fit beyond the obvious. One executive said, "If you are going to make the call, then be prepared. I often get people that say they thought they were going to get voice mail and weren't prepared to have a live conversation. That's no way to start a relationship." Universally, the best beginning to any live conversation is to simply ask the person if it is a good time to talk.

Voice mail is a way of life. Therefore, voice messages are an important part of the way we communicate. Below is an example of a message that one industry executive thought was effective. "Good morning (name), I am sorry to bother you. I know it is a crazy time for you as always but I want to introduce myself to you over the phone when you have a few minutes. I work for a minor league baseball team in Florida and even though my research of your marketing activities may or may not lead to a sponsorship immediately, I know that we may meet each other in the future and I would like to start a dialogue when you have time" (Migala, 2003).

All corporations handle sponsorship solicitation differently. The volume is tremendous. Some corporations get as many as 3,000 proposals per year (Seaver, 2004). Recently, many corporations have moved to web-based proposal submission procedures. General Motors has been using an electronic submission process since 1999. Through their in-house marketing agency GM*R Works, they require applicants to complete forms detailing pertinent information about the sponsorship opportunity. Miller Brewing Company also uses an in-house agency but adds a corporate software filter for their proposals.

Some have a localized decision network where the distributor in the area has the authority to make decisions related to sponsorship. In other cases, all sponsorship decisions must be approved at the corporate headquarters. One executive seeking a sponsorship deal, who had extensive experience in working with soft drink and beer sponsors, approached a camera company in the same manner. He knew that the soft drink and beer companies would not consider a sponsorship unless there was a considerable amount of support from local retailers and regional distributors. Unfortunately, after obtaining the backing of field offices for the camera manufacturer, he went to the corporate headquarters only to find that headquarters didn't like "the tail wagging the dog" (Ukman, 1991, p. 2).

A thorough investigation of the business structure is certainly warranted for each potential sponsor. Coca-Cola, for example, selects 95% of its sponsored events at the local level. So, a sport marketer should not send a proposal to Atlanta without enlisting the support of the local bottler. In 1998, both Coke and Pepsi warned high school sport programs that they would not deal with agents or agencies. If the schools were interested in establishing a partnership, they would have to deal directly with the local bottler. Their rationale was simple; they want all of the dollars that go into a deal to benefit the school directly. Their findings had shown that some agents required commissions as high as 40% (Coke and Pepsi, 1998). A thorough analysis of point-of-access alternatives is becoming more important as corporations are being deluged with requests and many are not accepting unsolicited sponsorship proposals.

Preparing a Cover Letter

Typically after a sport marketer has identified the appropriate point-of-access, one of the first steps is preparing a cover letter. Allen (1998) suggested that the cover letter sent with a sponsorship proposal can often make the difference between getting a sponsorship package read and getting a nice "thanks, but no thanks" letter. She suggests several trusted rules that should be followed when composing a cover letter (Allen, 1998):

1. Make sure that you send the letter to the proper person at the corporation. Spell their name correctly and list their appropriate title. If you don't know this information, call the company switchboard for assistance.
2. Use compelling terminology as opposed to less effective phrases. Examples include *measurable response, reinforce market position, increase market share, solidify client relationships, integrate marketing opportunities.*
3. Make sure that your letter is focused on individually tailored benefits for the recipient. Some of the letter can be from a template, but the body must be customized for each sponsor with benefits matched to sponsor needs.
4. Do not make overly general statements that cannot be supported by facts. For example, don't say, "all of the media outlets are excited about this event." Rather, you should indicate which specific media have agreed to cover the event.
5. Never shift the responsibility of follow-up to the sponsor ("I look forward to hearing from you"). Instead, thank the reader for their time and indicate that you will call them the following week for further discussions regarding the proposal.

Sponsorship Proposal Presentations

The following model (Figure 8-1) has been used extensively in many sales situations and seems to work exceptionally well in selling sponsorships. The model begins with establishing your credibility, moves to the identification of challenges, explains how the sponsorship can provide solutions, and concludes with the pricing information.

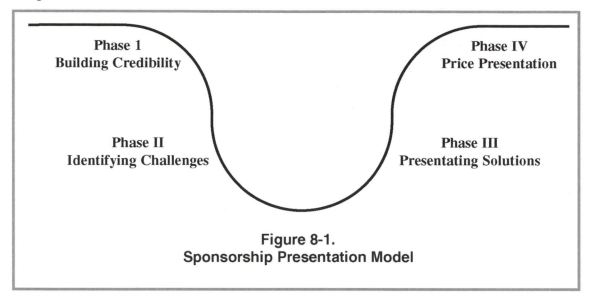

Figure 8-1.
Sponsorship Presentation Model

As mentioned in Chapter 3, corporations may be hesitant to allow their image, trademarks and brands to be managed by an unproven sport organization. Therefore, building credibility (Phase I) is essential in securing the corporation's trust. The advertising slogan of the first worldwide Olympic sponsorship program was "A Company Is Judged by the Company It Keeps." A multitude of factors can lead to the establishment of credibility including, business mannerisms, acceptable protocol, previous performance history, and testimonial evidence. Notwithstanding these factors, personal charm and charisma also contribute to building trust.

Phase II of the process involves an open review of challenges that the potential sponsor may face. The biggest mistake that properties make when presenting proposals to sponsors is focusing too much on what they have to sell, not on what the sponsor needs to buy. This relates to the marketing theory of product versus market orientation. People are more successful selling products (and sponsorships) that consumers are convinced they need, rather than whatever the salesperson is trying to sell. The challenges sponsors face are often associated with identifying and acquiring customers. The stages of buyer readiness referenced in many marketing texts indicate that buyers move through definable stages in the product adoption process (Pride & Ferrell, 1997). You can demonstrate to sponsors precisely how a sponsorship can address these challenges through the scenario depicted below.

Identification of Product Need

Example: Consumers can come to the realization that they have a need for a particular product if they see that product in use in the sport activity or at the event.

Quest for Information

Example: Sponsorships can provide information in the form of brochures, program advertisements, product displays, or public address announcements to assist consumers with their quest for increased product knowledge.

Product Evaluation

Example: Consumers may have information about a company's products, but may not have actually tried it. Through product sampling, sponsorships can allow consumers to evaluate the product before deciding to purchase. If a company has a new product, these activities can motivate consumers toward retail purchase.

Purchase of the Product

Example: Many sponsorship packages have used coupons as a means to drive sales. These tactics can move in two directions, first coupons can be made available at the event, or, second, sponsors can make discounted ticket coupons available at their retail outlets. Both of these methods have a good history of success. Some success has also been achieved through on-site sales activities.

Customer Satisfaction

Example: Most companies gather data on customer satisfaction. Sporting events can provide an excellent backdrop for these activities. You can set up areas for intensive focus group sessions with an array of customer types. This is an activity many sponsors find desirable.

It must be emphasized that the model does not encourage cross-over tactics. In other words, you should discuss all of the challenges before proceeding to the solutions segment (Phase 3) of the presentation. From a psychological standpoint, this will build momentum for closing the sale. Listening carefully to what the sponsor said during Phase II is critical in presenting the solutions. Some concerns frequently expressed by sponsors: "We need to activate our target audience." "We need a reputable partner." "Can you provide sampling opportunities?" "Additional media exposure is certainly desirable" (Stotlar, 2001).

All of these elements were identified as challenges that the NBA could address for Schick Razors through their Official Supplier status. Therefore, the NBA developed extensive product give-away programs at arenas. In the final analysis, Schick's product manager said, "it made sense demographically. The target of men 18-34 was a perfect match with NBA audiences" (Schlossberg, 1990, p. 1). Schick also capitalized on their association with the NBA and their target market by sponsoring 700 college Super Hoops tournaments, where the playoffs were conducted at NBA games. Many of Schick's corporate objectives, image enhancement, product trial, and hospitality tied directly to stages of consumer behavior and were accomplished through their NBA sponsorship.

Closing an agreement and obtaining the payment (Phase IV) is typically referred to as "The Ask." Many sport marketers are comfortable making presentations and discussing the virtues of the team or event. However, actually asking someone to hand over a check for $200,000 can be distressing. Negotiating the price of the sponsorship is also a formidable process. As with most business dealings, the physical setting for the negotiation is critical. One approach is to set up a face-to-face meeting, host it if possible, in order to create an opportunity to demonstrate hospitality (Just a hint: Don't pull a Coke out from the refrigerator during your meeting with Pepsi executives).

When the Phoenix Coyotes (NHL) scheduled a meeting with Bar S Foods to present sponsorship ideas for the coming season, they proceeded through all of the basic points and then invited the Bar S Foods executives into the front office. There they found about 90% of the Coyotes staff having a barbeque lunch, complete with Bar S hotdogs. The Bar S people commented, "Those types of personal touches mean so much and it has us leaving on such a high note" (Presenting sponsor, 2004). Hosting the meeting will also allow you to control the time better. Occasionally when you have a meeting scheduled at the sponsor's place of business, key executives may be delayed and end up usurping your time allotment.

During the presentation, avoid using any media that involves turning off the lights. It is important to watch the reactions of the audience during the presentation. Therefore, charts graphs and portfolios are usually better than slides or overheads. Computer-generated presentations are also excellent if they do not require the lights to be lowered. Remember, sometimes a marketer has to spend a bit on the presentation to make it effective. The owner of the NBA Denver Nuggets and NHL Colorado Avalanche spent $50,000 on their presentation to Pepsi for title sponsorship of the Pepsi Center in Denver. While the cost was substantial, the presentation was successful.

Negotiations

Negotiations must start with an offer and since the sport marketer is the one presenting the proposal, making the offer is always their responsibility. If the sport marketer has done the homework on pricing, the sponsorship should be valued correctly. However, most business executives will issue a counter-offer. First and foremost, the effective sport marketer acknowledges willingness to work with the proposing organization as a sponsor. Next, a strategy that has met with a lot of success is to review the benefits and price-value relationship previously presented. This often has the effect of reinforcing the message and can result in an agreement. If, however, they continue to suggest a price lower than the asking price, the sport marketer should reduce the sponsorship package and eliminate some of the associated benefits, in essence, offering them a diminished package. Another option would be to offer to locate a co-sponsor to share the costs. At times it is difficult to walk away from an offer. In 2002, the Arizona Diamondbacks (MLB) were coming off of a World Series Championship. They made a presentation to a sponsor priced at $1 million and the sponsor offered $600,000. They had clearly presented more than $1 million in value and had other sponsors in at that level, so they had to walk away from the deal. One of the primary reasons for rejecting the offer was to protect the integrity of their other partnerships (Brubaker, 2003). Ultimately, if a sponsor remains steadfast with their first offer after the sport marketer has reviewed the value and offered to find co-sponsors, then the meeting should be adjourned. The chances are marginal that an agreement will ever result. If the negotiations are successful and an agreement is reached, then the next step is to establish a timeline for contact finalization.

From the sponsor's side, industry veteran Ethan Green (2004) provided several useful tips for the negotiating process. He suggests that sponsors negotiate an Exit Clause. There are times when situations within the sponsoring company change or the sponsorship fails to deliver on its promised impact. Another clause that should be included is a performance clause. This would tie the sponsorship fee to the claims made by the organization in terms of event attendance, TV ratings, or other aspects of the agreement. Such a clause could set a window or conditions under which cancellation would be acceptable or fees reduced. Some sponsorships are directly tied to sales. For example, Gatorade signed a deal with Virginia Beach Parks & Recreation Department where Gatorade did not pay an upfront fee, but based their fee on product sales. They provided $6000 for the 1st 1,600 cases of Gatorade sold, $3000 for the next 1600, and $1000 for every additional 1600 cases sold. The entire sponsorship fee amounted to $15,000 over 3 years. Green also recommended that sponsors consider including exclusive items in the sponsorship package (also noted in Chapter 7). Sport organizations often have access to game-worn jerseys, autographed merchandise or other unique items. Sponsors could make valuable use of these items with their clients or employees.

Managing Sponsor Relationships

Managing any business relationship is predicated on the contract existing between the two parties. Sponsorship contracts are critical because many of the terms and concepts remain imprecise. Reed (1990) outlined some basic rationale for having a contract:

1. Contracts are needed to clarify the right assigned to the sponsor and specify the rights retained by the sport organization. Problems have sometimes occurred when sponsors attempted to assign some of their rights to another party. Specifically, Home Depot, one of the sponsors of the 1996 Atlanta Olympic Games, allowed suppliers (e.g. Black & Decker) to use the logo of the organizing committee on their products sold at Home Depot stores.

2. The contract should clearly define Title Sponsor, Official Supplier, Presenting Sponsor and other terms used in the relationship. These terms have no universal meaning or legal interpretation other than what is delineated in the contract.

3. A thorough contract will stipulate the size and placement of all event/ stadium signage. Detailed descriptions must be included prescribing the exact location and dimensions of all signage and assign the responsibility for manufacturing and erecting the signs.

4. Category exclusivity was noted in Chapter 3 as an important benefit. However, the boundaries of sponsor categories are unclear. For instance, does "financial services" cover banks and credit cards? Does it cover investment services? Considerable attention must be given to setting category parameters.

5. Contracts are also essential in clarifying the attendant liability of all parties involved. In most instances, sponsors will require that the sport entity include them as a co-insured on all insurance documents. Sponsors will not risk their corporate assets by exposing them through your failures, crises or mismanagement.

6. Protecting the event as an intellectual property is another reason for executing a contract. Several years ago, Coors Brewing Company served as title sponsor of the Coors Light Silver Bullet Biathlon Series. However, when it came time for renewal after two successful years of the event, Coors delivered a letter to the originators of the event that stated,

> While COORS will evaluate your proposal for possible use in the future it cannot make any commitments until all programs have been reviewed. . . . Please be advised that COORS may be developing similar or related projects, independent of any promotional ideas or proposals [XYZ] has submitted (Stotlar, 2001, p. 119).

A few weeks later, the organizer received notice that Coors would not be renewing its contract and had, in fact, hired one of the previous organizer's employees to stage an almost identical event for Coors. These types of actions can be reduced through a clause in the contract that restricts the sponsor from staging a similar event for a specified number of years. This is typically called a "covenant not to compete."

7. Contracts are also useful in establishing future rights as a sponsor. Because, in many instances, the full value of sponsorship is not realized in a single year, many sponsors would like to secure the opportunity to retain their sponsorship status. This has been termed the *right of first refusal*. This clause mandates that you offer future options to continuing sponsors before allowing competitors to sign-on. This does not restrict you from changing prices from year to year, but does provide the sponsor with the capacity to continue if their objectives are achieved. To extended benefits from sponsor relationships, most sponsors prefer to sign multi-year contract covering 3-5 years and obtain a right of first refusal.

Sport sponsorship represents a partnership, and protecting a sponsor's domain is in the sport marketer's best interest. Attending to these contractual details promotes mutual understanding prior to the implementation of a sponsorship alliance. Hopefully, such a relationship will serve the mutual needs of both parties and provide the desired benefits.

References

Allen, S. (1998). *Pitching with a Pen*. Holmdel, NJ: Allen Consulting, Inc.

Brubaker, S. (2003). Negotiations part one: Executives outline approach to say no to a prospective sponsor. *Team Marketing Report, 15*(4), 7.

Coke and Pepsi warn schools: No sponsorships via agents (1998, August 31). IEG *Sponsorship Report*, 1-2.

IEG survey finds sponsor pool growing more diverse. (2001, October 15). *IEG Sponsorship Report*, 1, 4-5.

Green, E. (2004). *Ethan Green's ten tips of improve sponsor negotiations*. Retrieved June 6 from http://www.migalareprot.com/june 04/negotitations.cfm.

Migala, D. (2003). *Turning cold calls into hot leads*. Retrieved November 4 from http://www.migalareport.com/nov03_story3.cfm.

Presenting sponsor: How to jazz up your sponsorship sales presentation (2004). Retrieved January 5, from http://www.migalareprot.com/jan04_story3.cfm.

Pride, W. M., and Ferrell, O. C. (1997) *Marketing*, 10th Edition. New York: Houghton Mifflin Company.

Reed, M. H. (1990). *Legal Aspects of Promoting and Sponsoring Events*. Chicago: International Events Group.

Schlossberg, H. (1990, April 2). Sports Marketing. *Marketing News*, p. 1.

Seaver, R. (2004, January). *2004 Corporate Sponsorship Survey Report*. San Diego: Seaver Marketing Group.

Stotlar, D. K. (2001). *Developing Successful Sport Marketing Plans*. Morgantown, WV: Fitness Information Technology.

Ukman, L. (1991, April 8). Assertions. Special Events Reports, 2.

Sponsorship Activation Worksheets

The worksheets provide a guide for developing various sections of a sponsorship plan. The following sheets cover the activation of the sponsorship. Complete these worksheets as a preparatory step in the creation of a sponsorship plan.

Draft a cover letter to the person responsible for sponsorship decisions at the sponsor's headquarters.

_____

_____

_____

_____

_____

_____

_____

_____

Develop an outline for your sponsorship proposal presentation.

_____

_____

_____

_____

_____

_____

_____

_____

_____

_____

_____

Structure your negotiation strategies, covering possible challenges from the sponsor.

_____

_____

_____

_____

_____

_____

_____

Delineate all administrative tasks for managing the sponsorship.

_____

_____

_____

_____

_____

_____

_____

_____

Chapter Nine

Managing Sport Sponsorships

Introduction

The sport organization, as the recipient of the sponsorship dollars has the responsibility of demonstrating the value received by the sponsor. First of all, Spoelstra (1997, p. 173) suggested, "Do whatever it takes to make the sponsorship successful." In his interviews and research with leading sponsors, Stotlar (1999) found that several sponsors reported that very few sport organizations followed up their partnership with either final reports or supporting data. The sponsorship manager for a major national banking firm indicated that in her 10 years of sponsorship management, only a handfull of event managers had submitted reports to her with supporting data. In contrast to this practice, most authorities maintain that information must be provided that shows an immediate return on the sponsorship investment for the company (Spoelstra, 1997; Stotlar, 1999).

Creating a Sponsorship Report

Spoelstra (1997) suggested that an annual report be delivered to each sponsor detailing the tangible benefits supplied. In its sponsorship contracts, General Motors requires "proof of performance" reports and fulfillment audits before final sponsorship payments are made. In this digital age, the Durham Bulls created their fulfillment report on CD-Rom giving sponsors a great opportunity to see, hear and experience what they got in return for their partnership with the team. One size does not fit all. Just like your sponsorship proposal, the fulfillment report needs to be customized for each sponsor. In line with this practice, the San Jose Sharks (NHL) are but one of the many professional teams that create a customized report for each sponsor detailing their involvement with the team.

Spoelstra also indicated that best practice would include samples of all sponsorship materials, or photos of sponsor images and signage in a "scrap book" format for graphic impression. Furthermore, the report should relate all of the promotional activities conducted to support the sponsorship. Not only would this make the company liaison feel good about their sponsorship decision, but it would also provide them with material to justify their actions within the sponsoring corporation. Amshay and Brian (1998) suggest that sponsors are increasingly demanding more sophisticated measurement of value. These measures typically parallel measures used to evaluate all corporate marketing elements. Spoelstra remarked, "prove it to the decision-makers' boss" (p. 172).

The problem exists because while sponsors want to know the exact return on their investment, sponsorship is difficult to measure. We have mistakenly applied standard advertising metrics to sponsorship measurement. While some of the measures are appropriate, others fail to capture the essence of sponsorship value in generating affective results in the mind and heart of the consumers (Ukman, 2004).

Measuring Return on Investment

While many corporate officers use ROI measurements to guide all of their business decisions, the rigidity of this approach leaves little room for flexibility. Sponsorship is not as easily quantified as some other business activities. There are certainly quantitative measures that can be employed, but qualitative measures also have their place.

From a quantitative standpoint, many event managers collect data on awareness and recall of sponsor's signage. Several examples of this type of data exist. Turco (1996) conducted research on college basketball fans, noting that more than 50% of fans were able to recognize sponsor's arena signage. Stotlar and Johnson (1989) found recognition rates of up to 70% in an earlier study of college sport venues. Pitts' (1998) investigation of sponsor recognition at the Gay Games IV indicated that participants were highly cognizant of sponsor identity. Her findings demonstrated that over 75% of participants were able to correctly name 3 of the 4 major sponsors, with 57.8% identifying the other. The data also pertain to the elusive GenY population. Bennett, Henson and Zhang (2002) noted that participants and attendees at action sports events (Gravity Games) were able to recognize the sponsors are an impressive 90% rate. These data would be critically important to sponsors and it is incumbent on sport managers to collect these types of data and report them to corporate partners.

Occasional problems can occur. What if data showed that no one saw the stadium signage? What if they couldn't remember it after they left the stadium? Exactly this scenario occurred in Stotlar and Johnson's (1989) research on stadium signage. At one institution, not one single fan surveyed could accurately remember one sign that appeared on the scoreboard. Should the sport organization tell the business that purchased it? First reactions may be to avoid communicating this fact to the sponsor, yet good business practices should mandate it. In reality, the sport organization may not know the specific reasons for their purchase. The company may have felt some affiliation with the university and would stay on as sponsor. There may also be a need to review decisions regarding color and graphics that affect the fans' response.

It is also important that consumers be able to recall the name of the sponsor whether that recollection was spurred by signage or not and contribute to marketing activities and positive consumer behavior. Data from the 2002 Winter Olympic games showed that 72% of people surveyed were able to recognize VISA as an Olympic sponsor. After the 2002 Winter Olympics, 20% of people who recognized VISA as an Olympic sponsor said that they used VISA more than the previous month. From its beginning as an Olympic sponsor, VISA's measure of consumer preference as "best overall card" has risen 50% through the 2000 Sydney Games. Their rank as "most accepted card" has doubled. Given that the credit card industry generates $1.1 trillion per year in US consumer spending, and $2.5 trillion worldwide, these increases in use preference would provide a substantial return on their investment (VISA USA, 2004; International Olympic Committee, 2002a; International Olympic Committee, 2002b).

Notwithstanding the success of VISA, Stotlar's (1993) research showed that, in general, few people could identify Olympic Sponsors. Most Olympic TOP sponsors had recognition rates of less than 20%. Only two sponsors were able to surpass 50% in consumer recognition as a sponsor. While the data may look dismal, we cannot jump to the conclusion that spectator recognition was the only (or even primary) motivation of the sponsor. For the Olympics, hospitality has been show to be a leading objective. In the long run, honesty and ethics must prevail. You never know, the sponsor may serve as a positive reference or make other purchases in lieu of the stadium ad. In this case, additional study and interviews would be warranted.

Seaver (2004) notes that a better term for assessment is Return on Objective (ROO) as opposed to Return on Investment. The principle supporting this approach is that a specified value can be placed on attaining a specific objective. Sport marketers could then assess the accomplishment of the objective. For example, a business-to-business objective to create more favorable opinions about a brand, the sponsor may include hospitality activities at an event. The objective measure (as employed by UPS and their NASCAR sponsorship) would be to track the shipping activities of the attendees against last year's volume. On the other hand, LG Electronics may be more interested in the perceptions of action sports participants that LG is a "cool" brand. Qualitative interviews with event participants would reveal the answer. The hope of LG is that eventually the "cool" factor would translate to increased sales. In the "best practice' section of this chapter is an example of LG's breakout of the return on objectives from an action sports event where they hope the "cool brand" image will be further enhanced. Similarly, some corporations that sponsor racing hope that the excitement of racing will transfer to their otherwise unexciting product. That is difficult to quantify. In experience marketing, companies want to create "touch points" with their customers. Qualitative research, including interviews and focus groups, are best used to measure these objectives.

Ukman (2004) outlined a basic process for collecting and reporting data to sponsors. She identified the first step in the process as setting objectives and baselines. "Articulating measurable objectives is a prerequisite of effective sponsorship measurement (Ukman, 2004, p. 3). The objectives should be directional, time framed, and audience specific. The second step in the process is creating the measurement plan. What types of data are needed to measure the above-stated objectives? Who will be responsible for collecting the data? These issues need to be clarified from the beginning of the sponsorship process. Benchmarks need to be established against which the data can be compared. If a 5% increase in sales is desired, sponsors must know the baseline to complete the analysis with post-event data. Data can be collected for multiple sources: employees, distributors, spectators, participants, vendors or the general public. Unfortunately, 86% of sponsors spend nothing or less than 1% of their sponsorship budget on measurement. Ukman's third step is implementation of the measurement plan. For example, if the measurement plan was to assess awareness, data such as those noted above on recall and recognition would be collected. However, if the objective were to evaluate brand loyalty, then data would need to be collected through audience surveys. Questions like "Would they recommend this brand to friends?" or "How likely would they be to use this brand?" would be appropriate. Finally, the fourth step in the process is to calculate the return on sponsorship. This includes assigning values to the measurement points in the plan. IEG, Sponsoraid and other corporations frequently provide benchmark data on the value of sponsorship elements. These are best when applied to discrete markets (Sponsoraid) but can also be provided on a national basis (IEG).

Sponsor Integration

To ensure the success of sponsorship partners, the sport marketer should assist sponsors with fully integrating their sponsorship activities within their company. Of primary concern is the understanding of the rationale for the sponsorship by company employees. Not just the marketing staff, but also all of the employees. Educating company employees by clarifying the objectives and the resulting benefits can enhance employee support for and involvement in sponsorship activities ("Five Key Factors," 2004).

Why Sponsors Drop Out

Sponsors cannot be counted on for an indefinite period; they often drop out, and for a variety of reasons. Sawyer (1998) identified some of the reasons that sponsors cited for withdrawing from sponsorship arrangements. Several sponsors mentioned a decrease in the market value of the event. This was determined either by reduced attendance at a particular event or by a drop in the television ratings. When the Women's United Soccer Association (WUSA) folded in 2003 they blamed their demise on lack of sponsorship. The reality was that the WUSA was pricing sponsorship beyond what could be expected in return for value. They were attempting to secure four major sponsors at $10 million each. A review of the opportunities did not show value anywhere near $10 million. This was not a sexist bias as some proposed, but rather an overpriced product in a market full of competitors. It also reinforces the notion that they were more interested in what they had to sell as opposed to what the sponsors might want to buy.

On occasion, the cost of sponsoring an event simply becomes prohibitive for the company. One illustration of this phenomenon was in tennis with sponsorship of the US Open. "So intertwined was Lipton with the event over the last 13 years that it has become known simply as 'The Lipton'" (Kaplan, 1998, p. 15). In many ways, the popularity of the event and tennis in general priced Lipton out of title sponsorship. With a price of $5 million, Lipton was on longer able to afford title sponsorship of the event. Furthermore, after 8 years of sponsorship with the Open, Pepsi dropped out. Pepsi executive noted, "The Open is a great hospitality vehicle, but the decision was based on us wanting to concentrate on sports properties that can do more as far as moving cases of soda" (Lefton, 2003, p. 12).

Another regularly cited explanation is a change in corporate direction. In other words, the company had decided that sport sponsorships were no longer in their best interests. One example of this factor was seen in Isuzu's decision to drop its sponsorship of the Celebrity Golf Challenge. Isuzu's vice president of marketing said "the sponsorship worked well for us for seven years, and our decision not to renew was predicated solely on a change of direction in which we were getting into more action-oriented, high-energy, high-endurance sports that we can transfer to the personality and image of our products" (Brockington, 1998. p. 3). Similarly, FedEx ended their 5-year sponsorship with CART "because our business objectives and their business had changed" (Altenburg, 2003).

Timing and scheduling during any year is an aspect over which the sport manager may have little control. Events and opportunities may come in conflict with other corporate advertising or sponsorship campaigns. This reason alone has left many sport organizers without sponsorship even though their data and proposals were attractive. Sawyer (1998) also found that while multiple factors and hard data were required to convince a sponsor to initiate a sponsorship, one negative attribute was sufficient to drop out.

Preventing Dropout

Ukman (2003, p. 2) stated the obvious when she said, "too many sponsorship program are dropped not because they don't have measurable value, but because the value was not measured." Giving service to sponsors can prevent dropout. As noted previously, Joyce Julius & Associates has as its main business the provision of the type of data that can demonstrate the value of sponsorship. Its analysis of television coverage of sporting events provides estimates of the advertising value of the appearance of corporate logos and product/corporate mentions by the announcers according to the time of on-screen presence. Supporting information should also be collected and provided by the sport organization. Factors such as attendance and crowd demographics are of particular importance to sponsors and are almost always readily available. Additional information on the psychographics, buying habits, attitudes, and loyalty of attendees is also critical for sponsors. The more you know about your event and its audience, the more power you will have in attracting and keeping sponsors.

Summary

As has been suggested, data needed to justify involvement in sport sponsorships is important to both the event owner and the sponsor. The best practice is to complete an accurate and extensive post-event report that details the value of the sponsorship. As a final note, if the sport marketer does not provide this information, the company executive who signed the $300,000 sponsorship check may not be employed when renewal comes around and they certainly won't be happy with a cancelled check as the only feedback on their investment. Hopefully, by following the guidelines and recommendations presented throughout this workbook, the reader will be successful in developing and implementing successful sport sponsorship plans of their own.

Best Practice

LG Electronics, a large Korean-based company known mostly for the cell phones but a producer of digital appliances and flat screen TVs was title sponsor of the 2003 LG Action Sports Championships held in Los Angeles. Below you will find information ranging from their objectives to the post-event measurement activities. The key points in this case include LG's integration, activation, and measurement practices.

2003 LG Action Sports Championships
LG Objectives
1. To increase brand awareness and create familiarity between LG and the target audience in action sports and music through pre-event marketing initiatives and on-site activation.
2. Build a compelling interactive experience to engage the target audience in a personal and memorable way so that LG's sponsorship will remain with the consumer long after the event is over.

Event Data

Attendance- 31,368; 45% in the 15-17 age group; 73% have a cell phone and the remainder have a high intend to purchase.

Sales Potential

Potential LG cell phone purchases- 25% of attendees will purchase in the next year (8,000) and the average price of a phone is $200. 2,640 were either likely or somewhat likely (discounted 50%) to purchase LG. Therefore the market sales potential is $528,000.

Key Marketing Elements

Pre event TV
> 75- 30 sec. Placements generating 1.2 million impressions valued at $303, 400 Road to the LG Action Sports Championships- 60 min feature 399,000 placements values at $72,000.

Pre event On-line
> LG "Pic Trick" voting at web site, and randomly drawn product give a ways. 3,796 voters from 4,662 unique visitors valued at $8,400

On-site Activation
> LG Lounge
> VIP hospitality
> Music stage
> LG Phone girls
> Pic Trick sweepstakes
> Enter to win raffle
> Athlete appearances
> Product demonstration kiosks
> "Name That Tone" game
> LG cell phone inflatables
> Participant gift packs with LG products and logo souvenirs

References

Altenburg, N. (2003). Negotiations part one: Executives outline approach to say no to a prospective sponsor. *Team Marketing Report*, 15, (4), 7.

Amshay, T. & Brian, V. (1998, July 20-26). Sport sponsorship sword cuts both ways. *Sports Business Journal*, 23.

Bennett, g. Henson, R. & Zhang, J. (2002). Action sports sponsorship recognition. *Sport Marketing Quarterly*, 11 (3), 25-34.

Brockington, L. (1998, September 21-27). Isuzu drops tourney sponsorship. *Sports Business Journal*, 3.

Five key factors that ensure relevant activation and sponsorship success (2004). *IEG Sponsorship Report*, 23 (11), 1-3.

International Olympic Committee (2002a). *Marketing Fact File.* Lausanne; International Olympic Committee.

International Olympic Committee (2002b). *Salt Lake 2002 Marketing Report.* Lausanne; International Olympic Committee.

Kaplan, D. (1998, September 7-13). Lipton to bow out of title sponsorship. *Sports Business Journal*, 15.

Lefton, T. (2003, October 6-12). Pepsi out as sponsor of US Open tennis. *Sports Business Journal*, 12.

Pitts B. G. (1998). An analysis of sponsorship recall during Gay Games IV. *Sport Marketing Quarterly*, 7, 4, 11-18.

Sawyer, L. (1998). *Why Sponsors Drop Out.* Boston: National Sports Forum.

Seaver, R. (2004, January). *2004 Corporate Sponsorship Survey Report.* San Diego: Seaver Marketing Group.

Spoelstra, J. (1997). *Ice to the Eskimos.* New York: Harper Business.

Stotlar, D. K. (1993). Sponsorship and the Olympic winter games. *Sport Marketing Quarterly*, 2,3, 35-46.

Stotlar, D. K. (1999). Sponsorship in North America: A survey of sport executives. *Journal of Sport Marketing and Sponsorship.* 1, (1), 87-100.

Stotlar, D. K. and Johnson, D. M. (1989, July). Assessing the impact and effectiveness of stadium advertising on sport spectators at division one institutions." *Journal of Sport Management*, 3 (2), 90-102.

Turco, D. M. (1996). the effects of courtside advertising on product recognition and attitude change. *Journal of Sport Management*, 5, 4, 11-15.

Ukman, L. (2003). Assertions. *IEG Sponsorship Report*, 22, (21), 2.

Ukman, L. (2004). *Return on Sponsorship.* Chicago: International Events Group.

Visa USA making the most of 2004 Olympic Games with marketing campaign. (2004, March 31. San Francisco: Visa USA, press release.

Management Worksheets

The worksheets provide a guide for developing various sections of a sponsorship plan. The following sheets cover the management of the sponsorship including the final report to the sponsor. Complete these worksheets as the culmination of sponsorship activities.

Identify the person responsible for sponsor services.

_____

_____

Complete the Post-Event Report

List the event date:

Report the attendance:

Calculate the audience (immediate and mediated numbers)

_____

_____

_____

_____

_____

Report the demographic profile of the audience.

_____

_____

_____

_____

Specify the media coverage & compute the commercial value attained.

_____

_____

_____

_____

_____

_____

_____

Record the impressions/recognition data for all sponsorship elements.

_____

_____

_____

_____

_____

_____

Record the qualitative data for appropriate sponsorship elements.

_____

_____

_____

_____

_____

_____

Prepare the final report for the sponsor (as applicable)

_____

_____

_____

_____

_____

_____

_____

_____

Index

Businesses and Products Index

Clubs, Events, Leagues, and Teams Index

Athletes and Celebrities Index

Author

David K. Stotlar, Ed.D.
Professor, Sport Management, School of Sport & Exercise Science, University of Northern Colorado
B.A. Eastern Illinois ('74), M.S. Slippery Rock ('76), Ed.D. Utah ('80)

Dr. David K. Stotlar teaches on the University of Northern Colorado faculty in the areas of sport marketing and sponsorship. He has had over sixty articles published in professional journals and has written several textbooks and book chapters in sport management and marketing. He has made numerous presentations at international and national professional conferences. On several occasions, he has served as a consultant in sport management to various sport professionals; and in the area of sport marketing and sponsorship, to multinational corporations and international sport managers. David was selected by the USOC as a delegate to the International Olympic Academy in Greece and the World University Games Forum in Italy and served as a venue media center supervisor for the 2002 Olympic Games. He has conducted international seminars in sport management and marketing for the Hong Kong Olympic Committee, the National Sports Council of Malaysia, Mauritius National Sports Council, the National Sports Council of Zimbabwe, the Singapore Sports Council, the Chinese Taipei University Sport Federation, the Bahrain Sport Institute, the government of Saudi Arabia, the South African National Sports Congress and the Association of Sport Sciences in South Africa. Dr. Stotlar's contribution to the profession includes an appointment as Coordinator of the Sport Management Program Review Council (NASPE/NASSM) from 1999-2001. He previously served as Chair of the Council on Facilities and Equipment of the American Alliance for Health, Physical Education, Recreation and Dance and as a Board Member and later as President of the North American Society for Sport Management. Dr. Stotlar was a member of the initial group of professionals inducted as NASSM Research Fellows. He is also a founding member of the Sport Marketing Association.